Contents

Preface

Part 1 General appearance *1*
1. Appearance *1*
2. Qualities *6*
3. The reception area *14*
4. Business organization *17*

Part 2 Sources of information *21*
5. Reference books *21*
6. Teletext and Viewdata *26*
7. Other sources of reference *29*

Part 3 Reception routines *32*
8. Appointments and diaries *32*
9. Visual aids *35*
10. Reminder systems *39*
11. Flower arranging *42*
12. Entertaining *45*
13. Receiving parcels and messages *48*
14. Safety and fire precautions *52*
15. First aid *57*

Part 4 Communications *60*
16. Telephone services and their use in business *60*
17. Telephone equipment *64*
18. Telephone technique *69*
19. Routing calls *74*
20. Other methods of communication *77*

Part 5 Business procedures *82*
21. The post *82*
22. Banking and current account procedures *87*
23. Petty cash *92*
24. Filing and indexing *96*
25. Calculating machines *100*
26. Wages and salaries *102*

Index *106*

Preface

This book has been written to prepare students for the Royal Society of Arts Certificate in *General Reception*. It is also eminently suitable for the Business Education Council's option module specification *Receptionist/Telephonist* at BEC General level.

There are questions at the end of each chapter and a series of assignments, which are suitable for the BEC module, are also incorporated into the book.

H. Atkins

Acknowledgements

The Publisher wishes to thank the following for permission to reproduce copyright material: The Controller of Her Majesty's Stationery Office; National Westminster Bank Limited and The Post Office.

Part 1
General appearance

1 Appearance

The receptionist, as the name implies, is the person who receives visitors and clients on behalf of her firm. She answers their queries, directs or deals with their complaints and attends to their requirements. She is able to refuse requests without giving offence and will use diplomacy and tact in difficult and awkward situations.

She is the 'front line' representative of her firm. The first impression that the visitor will receive when entering the offices of any organization is that given by the receptionist. Good human relationships are built up mainly through the impressions that each person makes on another. A bright, friendly, well-mannered receptionist will enable visitors to view the firm with esteem and respect.

The main impact of first impressions is that of appearance. The receptionist should endeavour to stay neat and well-groomed, no matter how busy and hectic her day. When visitors arrive at a reception area to find a receptionist wearing stained and shabby clothing, scuffed shoes and untidy hair then the first impression of the firm would be extremely unfavourable. The visitor would feel that a receptionist who looked so uncared for and uncaring could not be efficient and, it follows, that a firm that employed inefficient personnel would probably be inefficient in all its areas. The visitor could lose faith in the firm's products and services and irreparable harm would be done.

A neat well-groomed appearance does not come about by mere chance. This must be planned for. It comes basically from being scrupulously clean – hair, hands, teeth, nails and skin. This scrupulous cleanliness of hair, hands, teeth, nails and skin applies equally to the male receptionist who is now employed in many organizations. His choice of clothing should be in accordance with his working environment and his duties. An hotel receptionist is usually required to wear collar and tie with or without a jacket, depending upon formality, the size and the situation of the hotel. The male receptionist in a hairdressing salon may wear casual clothes whereas, the male receptionist in large local government offices is often required to wear a neat, conservative uniform.

It is, therefore, impossible to state that a receptionist must dress in a particular way and this applies, even more so, to female receptionists. The appearance of the female receptionist in a large West End beauty parlour could be quite unsuitable for the receptionist who worked in a solicitor's office in a small town. There are, however, certain points to which all receptionists must give attention.

Posture

Good posture means that an individual will walk, sit and stand without slouching. Good posture gives a better figure and practising this is also excellent exercise. The way in which individuals hold their body will eventually influence its shape and, although the effect is slow, it is a steady changing process. Many figure faults began with bad posture in adolesence and can, in extreme cases, cause joint thickening and bone displacement. In less severe cases it produces sagging stomachs and buttocks as well as a thickened waistline and a 'paunch'.

When the back is held correctly the spine has an easy alignment. When the spine is out of alignment, due to poor posture, it produces a hollow back and squeezes the vertebrae together which leads to slipped discs and muscular pains in the back. The habit of holding oneself well will create an impression of confidence and vitality. The receptionist will also feel springier and less tired after a busy day and that alone is surely worth the effort involved in adopting a good posture and maintaining it.

Hair

The receptionist's hair should always look clean and free from any hint of grease. Hair that bounces, shines and has a look of vitality and control is the outcome of a programme of correct care.

Careless washing may be harmful if the wrong type of shampoo is used or if it is used in the wrong way. Modern shampoos are very concentrated and if too much is used it stimulates the oil glands resulting in greasy hair. After wetting the hair thoroughly a teaspoonful of shampoo should be sufficient to produce a good lather. Regular conditioning is a protective measure for hair and will restore hair that has been damaged by too much tinting or perming.

One of the most irritating hair disorders is that of dandruff. The receptionist who suffers from this disorder needs to combat it in two ways.
1 Keeping the scalp clean by frequent washing and by using one of the medicated shampoos especially produced for reducing dandruff. The hair must be thoroughly rinsed and a teaspoonful of antiseptic may be added to the final rinse.
2 Watching the diet and refusing to eat too much sugar and starch as this leads to the acidity which causes the noticeable white flakes near the roots of the hair.

Whatever the length of hair it should be trimmed every 6–7 weeks. Hair should never be allowed to just grow as this produces split ends and an untidy appearance. Cutting the hair should be done only by the expert, as well-cut hair is the basis of all successful hair styles, those that suit the shape of the face.

If the receptionist's hair is untidy then the receptionist, no matter how well-groomed otherwise, is going to look untidy. If the receptionist is unable to manage her own hair then she should try to budget for regular visits to a hairdressing salon. Simple styles are ideal for the busy receptionist as elaborately dressed hair needs constant attention.

Hands

A receptionist's hands are always on show. What use is a beautifully made-up face, framed by clean, well-cut hair if the hands are red and rough with badly bitten nails?

Hands need special care as they are one of the driest parts of the body. Detergents, the sun and the cold take their toll and so it is important that the receptionist gives them daily care and protection. Rubber gloves should be worn for all work with water and every time hands get wet they should be dried thoroughly and hand cream should be applied. Once a week it is a good idea to massage the hands with a rich, oily cream.

Nails become brittle if they are exposed to extreme cold, too much sun or cleaning chemicals and cutting with scissors only encourages the splits and fractures. Nails should be filed to an oval shape with an emery board and should not be filed too deeply at the sides. Cuticles should be kept soft by keeping them well moisterised, then gently pushed back with a towel or a tissue. Nail polish protects and strengthens the nails but will only look beautiful if carefully applied. It must always be kept immaculate as chipped nail varnish looks very slovenly.

Skin care and make-up

Generally speaking, most women wear make-up to work. Usually, a natural look is the one to aim for, with make-up used to enhance the receptionist's face rather than stun the caller. The amount and style is the individual's choice but is also dependent upon the type of organization for which she works. The choice of make-up is a very individual one, the selection is vast, not only in the compounds but in the price. The receptionist should use what suits *her* skin. Generally the foundation shade that is closest to her skin tone is the best, and the darker her skin the more transparent-looking foundation should be. Foundation, whatever the shade, should always be used sparingly.

Eyes give a face much of its personality and it is fashionable to emphasize the eyes. It is possible to shade out the less attractive points and to highlight the attractive ones. This is achieved by using false eyelashes, eye shadow, eye lightener, eye liner and mascara. It is up to the receptionist to decide how much eye make-up to use but remember that heavily made-up eyes may look marvellous on an evening out but in most reception areas they are out of place.

Eyebrows give expression to a face and it is a mistake to alter their basic look. Some eyebrows have been so heavily plucked that the possessor looks permanently surprised. Eyebrows do, however, require some grooming to prevent them from looking straggly.

The receptionist should ensure that all her make-up is removed by a cleanser as stale make-up clogs the pores and produces skin problems such as blackheads and spots. A skin freshener does an important job in disposing of all traces of cleanser and pore dirt. Fresheners also help to stimulate circulation and refine the skin texture. This leaves the skin thoroughly cleansed and ready for the make-up.

Feet

Feet need regular care as well as hands. Shoes should be comfortable to wear, for aching feet may well make a receptionist less friendly and pleasant than she might otherwise be.

Daily care for the feet goes a long way towards ensuring that a receptionist's day is never ruined by tired or painful feet. She should:

1 Scrub feet daily with a stiff bristle brush;
2 Pumice any callouses or hard areas;
3 Massage feet with hand lotion;
4 Powder feet, as this helps to absorb moisture.

Nearly all foot trouble is caused by wearing the wrong sort of shoes – too high, too pointed or too small. Shoes should never be purchased with the idea that they will stretch after being worn for a while. Stockings should also be checked for size. If they are too tight or too small they lead to the same foot problems as tight shoes, namely corns, callouses and bunions. If a receptionist's feet hurt then she should, ideally, go to a chiropodist so that the problems may be dealt with by a professional.

Clothes

So much depends upon the receptionist's preference, her age, her shape and her budget that it would be difficult to say what she should, or should not wear. Generally though, clothes should be neat and clean, well brushed and the colours should not be too startling. As with the male receptionist – it depends on the duties and the environment. A doctor's receptionist may be required to wear a white coat, whereas, a receptionist in a multi-national organization may need to wear a well-cut coat and skirt. A receptionist in an advertising agency may be quite acceptable to callers and to her firm when dressed in jeans and a sweater. The receptionist must decide what is suitable for her particular job and dress accordingly.

General hygiene

The receptionist, who for so much of her time is in direct contact with the public, needs to make absolutely certain of personal freshness. Most people believe that body odour is caused by perspiration but this is not true. Perspiration is colourless and odourless. When it appears upon the skin it consists only of water and a little salt. What causes perspiration to smell unpleasantly is the bacteria which decompose moisture and turns it into an offensive body odour. This will only happen if the perspiration is left upon the skin long enough for decomposition to take place.

Most areas of the skin perspire but usually cause no body odour as the perspiration evaporates fairly quickly. The problem areas are the underarms, feet and pubic areas. All-over perspiration is adequately combated by taking regular baths or showers. The problem areas need special care. There are many deodorants for underarms, feet and pubic areas which will combat body odour by slowing down the action of the bacteria.

Anti-perspirants are slightly different to deodorants as they, besides fighting the bacteria, reduce the volume of perspiration. How well anti-perspirants and deodorants cope with body odour depends upon many variables:

1 *Clothes* Synthetic materials such as nylon hinder evaporation. If the receptionist is inclined to perspire heavily then she should try to ensure that her underwear, blouses, shirts etc are made from a natural material such as cotton. Natural fibres allow air to circulate and thus allows the perspiration to evaporate.

2 *Temperature* If the reception areas are centrally heated and not exposed to icy draughts each time doors are opened then the receptionist is bound to feel fairly warm during her working day.
3 *Exertion* Is the reception area a busy stimulating place with a constant stream of visitors?
4 *Tension* Does the receptionist have to deal with awkward customers and problem situations as a general rule rather than finding them an exception in an otherwise ordinary working day?
5 *Nature* Does the receptionist naturally perspire lightly or heavily?

All these factors will have a direct bearing on the volume of perspiration, but however little adults may perspire they ALL need to use deodorants or anti-perspirants to some degree. The receptionist must ensure that her choice is adequate for her needs.

Deodorants and anti-perspirants are only effective when applied to a thoroughly *clean* area, so they must never be used as a substitute for showers and baths. Chlorophyl has a marked effect on the bacteria that cause body odour so green vegetables eaten regularly will act as a natural deodorant.

Mouth odour

Most unpleasant mouth odours come from insufficiently clean teeth and sometimes from decaying teeth. Everyone should have a six-monthly check-up at the dentist. All cavities should be filled as early as possible and the teeth should be cleaned and descaled. Teeth should be thoroughly cleaned at least twice a day. Toothbrushes should have soft, thin bristles and be replaced every two or three months. Dental floss may be used to clean between the teeth where toothbrushes are unable to reach.

The breath may be freshened by using hydrogen peroxide as this kills oral bacteria and strengthens the gums. Receptionists should be aware that highly flavoured foods such as onions and garlic taint the breath for some hours after being eaten. This mouth odour may be disguised by eating peppermints, although it is a good idea for the receptionist to avoid highly flavoured foods during her working day. Occasionally bad breath is a symptom of some underlying stomach disorder. If the receptionist suspects that she has mouth odour in spite of taking all normal precautions she should consult her doctor.

Questions

1. What is the difference between an anti-perspirant and a deodorant?
2. Why is the receptionist called the 'front line representative of her organization'?
3. What are the two positive advantages of working to acquire good posture?
4. Name four important points in the care of the hair.
5. Why is a sensible diet important if a receptionist suffers from dandruff?
6. State what you think might be suitable clothing for the following:
   a) a receptionist at a beauty parlour;
   b) a receptionist at a dental surgery;
   c) a receptionist in a building society;
   d) a receptionist in an advertising agency?
7. Give four points to remember in caring for the feet.
8. What factors affect the degree of perspiration?
9. Why is regular care for the hands very important, especially for the receptionist?
10. What can the receptionist do to guard against halitosis?

Assignment 1

A receptionist's appearance is extremely important. Scrupulous cleanliness of hair, hands, teeth, nails and skin is essential.

You are a busy receptionist in a large company and you must remain calm throughout the busy, sometimes hectic, day.

1. Write down ten tips that will help you to stay fresh and unflustered from the beginning to the end of the working day.
2. Give your personal morning routine for 'all-day' personal freshness.
3. Design an outfit, including the shoes, that you think would be suitable for a receptionist in a medium-sized manufacturing company. You may use cut-outs or photographs if you wish.

2 Qualities

Apart from her appearance the receptionist's attitude to visitors is extremely important.

Welcoming visitors

When a visitor approaches the reception area the receptionist should always smile directly at the visitor and greet him or her followed with the words 'Can I help you Sir (or Madam)?' The receptionist's first question to callers should then be to ask their name. Once she knows this she should use it as it immediately makes the receptionist appear a friendly, welcoming person. The receptionist's name is very often displayed usually as a brooch which she will wear on her dress, though, she may have her name displayed on a desk stand in front of her.

Under no circumstances should a receptionist ignore her visitor while chatting to a colleague or while continuing with a trivial task. Even if she is talking on the telephone she may smile at the visitor to acknowledge his or her presence and indicate that she will give her full attention as soon as she is able.

Visitors may have travelled some distance to reach the organization and could be a little travel-weary and uncomfortable. They will be grateful if the receptionist takes their coats and umbrellas and shows them where the cloakroom is situated so they may freshen up.

If the member of staff with whom the visitor has an appointment is not immediately available then the visitor should be seated and not left propped up against the reception desk while the receptionist carries on with other tasks.

An exchange of light conversation is often welcomed by a visitor who may well be a stranger in the area. The obvious topic of conversation, the weather, may be explored and the sort of journey that the visitor has experienced. The visitor may wish to know one or two points about the firm but the receptionist should never divulge confidential information or be indiscreet in any way. Neither should she pry into the visitor's affairs. She should respond if callers comment on a major event of the day but it is neither the time nor the place for personal opinions nor for political discussions.

At the beginning of each day the receptionist should be informed of the appointments for the day. She may obtain information on the movements of the various members of staff so that she may act promptly when visitors arrive. Some firms keep a reception register. This provides a permanent record of every caller to the firm. This, however, is only usual in large firms and the smaller organizations may find that they are not necessary.

A reception register should contain the following information:

1. The date;
2. The caller's company;
3. The name of the caller;
4. The reason for the call;
5. The name of the caller's contact within the firm;
6. Whether the caller has an appointment;
7. The time of the appointment;
8. The time that the caller left.

Reception Register			Jones Brothers & Company Ltd			Date 22 October	
Name	Company	Reason for call	Contact	Appoint.	Time of arrival	Time of leaving
L Brush	Office Aids	To demonstrate new office copier	Mr Sinclair	yes	0930	1015
G Smith	Smith & Robinson	To arrange for annual audit	Mr Sutherland	yes	0945	1000
M Noble	Danes Shipments	To request stronger packing materials	Mr Blair	no	1015	1115
J Jones	Bells Advertising Agency	To arrange for new advertising copy	Mr Good	yes	1015	1130
Mrs L Ashe	39 Boxhill Rd Brighton	Applicant for position of accounts clerk	Mr Brinn	yes	1030	1100
D Dodson	Dodson Electrics	To discuss new wiring for main production shop	Mr Haines	yes	1030	1215
M Smart	15 Stert St Abingdon	Applicant for post of accounts clerk	Mr Brinn	yes	1115	1135
F Pearson	Dunstones Ltd	To arrange for new contract for supplying engine parts	Mr Cleary	yes	1115	1225
J Harris	124 Ferndale Rd Oxford	Applicant for post of accounts clerk	Mr Brinn	yes	1145	1210
L Holms	Jay Advertising	To sell advertising space	Mr Good	no	1145	Asked to write in for appoint.

Figure 1   Entries in a reception register

Quite often when a caller approaches the receptionist a business card may be presented. This gives details of:

1 His company;
2 His company's business;
3 The name of the representative with whom the receptionist is dealing;
4 The company's address and telephone number.

This is very useful to the receptionist for checking the spelling, company representative's name and business. The business card may also be useful to the receptionist when making introductions.

The doctor's or dentist's receptionist will need to check her appointments book for confirmation of the caller's name and time of appointment or making an appointment to see the doctor or dentist. Callers with appointments will then usually wait in the reception area or waiting-room until the doctor or dentist is ready to see them. The receptionist is usually responsible for ensuring that the patient's notes, case histories or charts are given to the doctor or dentist prior to the patient's consultation.

Figure 2   A business card

	Dr. Martin	Dr. Johnson	Dr. Dale	Dr. Mann
0915	Mrs Sloggett	Miss P Hill	–	L. Dodd
0930	John Julian	Mr R Martin	–	L P Jordan
0945	Mrs D Brown	Jean and John Collins	–	S F Stimpson
1000	Mr F Tucker	Mr R Shaw	P Bennett	Mrs P Bray
1015	–	Mrs F Spence	Mrs N Mckay	Mr T Bray
1030	–	S P Partridge	W T Russell	L Brill
1045	–	L F Manders	F Sutherland	S Partington
1100	–	–	P Haines	
1115	–	–	S Wilson	

Figure 3   Doctors' appointments book

Hotel Tregay		Register of Guests		
Date	Name	Nationality	Home address	Signature
18.8.81	John Adams	British	63 Adams Row LONDON WC1	
18.8.81	Sydney Brown Coral Brown	Irish Irish	16 Cork Street DUBLIN Ireland	
18.8.81	Sebastian Clark	British	The Vicarage Maltravers Whyde SUTTON Worcs	
18.8.81	Joan Darch	British	15 Rye Street St Anthony Abingdon OXON	
18.8.81	Ellis D. Jones Stella Jones	American American	1493 West Thirteenth Los Angeles USA	
18.8.81	Jerry Robins	British	16 Coach Road BRIGHTON	
18.8.81	Flora Lewes	British	The Cedars Park Road Swansea	
18.8.81	D.J. Brinn	British	44 Colwyn Drive LIVERPOOL	
18.8.81	Roy Powers Betty Powers	British	39 Boxhill Road Hamble SOUTHAMPTON	
18.8.81	Jean le Sais	French	16 Rue de la Paix CHERBOURG France	

Figure 4   Entries in a listed register

An hotel receptionist will have to verify that the caller has made a reservation. If he or she has no reservation then the receptionist may be required to allocate a suitable room, if one is available. Before the guest is conducted to the room the hotel register must be signed which gives a record of guests in the same way that a reception register gives a record of callers to a firm.

The modern trend, however, is for individual cards to be employed in reception as these offer more security and are not open to the general view.

Callers who have appointments usually present no problems to the receptionist.

In a large organization the receptionist will usually contact the secretary of the required

Hotel Tregay	Registration Card
Name	
Home address	
....	
Date	Room Number ....
Passport No.	
Nationality	
Signature	

Figure 5   A registration card

member of staff who will then collect the visitor herself and conduct him to the correct room. Occasionally, however, members of staff may leave messages with the receptionist that they are to be informed as soon as a visitor arrives and may, in these cases, collect the visitor personally.

Introductions

Sometimes the receptionist is expected to accompany the visitor to the office of the appropriate member of staff. There she should introduce the visitor clearly and give the name and the company. Rules for introducing people are extremely simple but a receptionist may, in the heat of the moment, forget the rules and find herself in a muddle. If this happens then the business card mentioned proves useful as a receptionist may, if necessary, read from the card when performing the necessary introductions.

Rules

1 Men are introduced to women.
2 Junior staff are introduced to executives.
3 Everyone is introduced to notabilities such as Members of Parliament and titled people.
4 A short designation of the person who is being introduced should be given.

Examples
1 'Miss Golightly, may I introduce Mr Frank Dobson, a candidate for the post of Sales Representative. Miss Marigold Golightly.'
2 'Mr Evans, may I introduce Mr Peter Warde, who is the new junior in our Accounts Department. Mr George Evans.'
3 'Sir Robert, may I introduce Miss Marigold Golightly who is our personnel officer. Sir Robert Jamieson.'

When introducing titled visitors it is as well to ensure that the correct form of address is employed. For example, when introducing a duke to a senior member of staff the receptionist should say:
'Your Grace, may I introduce Mr John Evans who is our Chief Accountant. His Grace, the Duke of Berkshire'.

The receptionist should endeavour to obtain a copy of the reference book *Black's Titles and Forms of Address*. This contains information on all forms of address, spoken and written, to members of the peerage, the church, privy counsellors, presidents of societies and even Scottish and Irish chieftains.

In smaller organizations the introductions may be a little less formal if Christian names are used among the staff as a general rule. The receptionist may, therefore, find that her introductions will follow a similar format to the following.

'Marigold, this is Frank Dobson who has come for an interview for the position of Sales Representative. Mr Dobson, Miss Marigold Golightly, our Personnel Officer.'

Correct introductions are essential in business life so that each party knows precisely to whom they are speaking, the designation of each and the reason for the call. The parties concerned may then get down to the business at hand. The receptionist here is acting in her capacity as intermediary, smoothing the path of the caller and also that of her employer.

Visitors often become irritated when their names are mispronounced. A receptionist *does* need to have a good memory for names and faces. Practice and concentration while names are given will help. It is not, however, always practicable for a receptionist to act as an escort particularly if she is in charge of a busy reception office or combines the job of receptionist with that of a telephonist.

Visitors without appointments

If a visitor calls without an appointment he or she is usually willing to wait until the appropriate person is available. The receptionist should ask the visitor to be seated and offer some company literature or a magazine. She should give her visitor the reason for any delay and keep him or her informed as to progress being made. Sometimes a visitor's call is particularly inconvenient and it is impossible for anyone to see them that day. The receptionist should make an appointment for another day but only after consultation with the appropriate member of staff. On occasion it is possible to suggest that the visitor sees another member of staff who is available and is able to deputise for the person required.

Black listed callers

Some callers have been 'black listed' by the management. This usually means that at some time in the past they have been nuisances to busy members of staff of the firm for the following reasons:

1 *Time wasting* Some visitors with no sense of 'time being money' will ramble endlessly and without point and, even after long discussion, find that they are unable to reach any decision.

2 *Pressurised selling* Salesmen are sometimes over-persuasive in their efforts to sell their company's products. They will not take 'NO' for an answer and will continue to 'over-sell' their goods long after the executive concerned has lost interest and patience.

3 *Petty complaints* Some customers complain about rather petty issues. They will soon become known to the management and the receptionist may well be asked to 'black list' callers such as these.

The receptionist will have a list of the names of such callers. Sometimes, in fact, she will need no list as these individuals are usually frequent visitors and become well-known to her. She must be courteous and as tactful as ever but must 'block' all their demands to see the required member of staff. She may ask them to leave messages or write letters so that they feel that they are receiving *some* attention. They must, however, be dealt with very firmly and with no hesitation or weakness whatever their arguments and explanations.

Some companies have a definite policy for all sales representatives:

1 No sales representatives may be seen without a definite appointment or
2 All sales representatives without appointments must wait until the Purchasing Manager is free to see them or
3 Only sales representatives with whom the company has had previous dealings will be seen without appointments.

Tact

The telling of small falsehoods is part of the receptionist's job.

'I am very sorry Mr Jeffrey but I am afraid that Mr Blair has been called away on urgent business. He wishes me to apologise on his behalf and wonders if you would like to make another appointment to see him. Alternatively you could see Mr Kenneth Parker who is Mr Blair's deputy. Mr Parker is familiar with your products and will be able to help you.'

How different was the message that the receptionist *really* received!

'Oh – darn it! I can't see old Jeffrey now, he never stops talking! Try to get Ken Parker to see him!'

How thoroughly offended Mr Jeffrey would be if the receptionist had delivered Mr Blair's message verbatim. As it is, he will probably be quite content to see Mr Parker and everyone will be happy. Tact is an essential quality for the successful receptionist. The receptionist also needs to protect members of staff from the possibility of unwelcome visitors. When Mr Smithers, who has arrived without an appointment, announces that he wishes to see Mr Blair, the receptionist does not announce via the telephone to Mr Blair:

'Mr Smithers from Mountjoys is here to see you Mr Blair.'

Instead she will say:

'Mr Smithers from Mountjoys would like to see Mr Blair if he is available.' This gives Mr Blair the chance to decide whether he is 'in' or 'out' to Mr Smithers.

In the same way if at the moment she saw Mr Blair crossing the foyer she would not call out:

'Mr Blair, there is someone here to see you.'

Mr Blair might be too busy to see a caller at that moment and this sort of situation which can easily be avoided, becomes embarrassing to everyone concerned.

Office organization

A receptionist needs to have a thorough knowledge of her organization. She should know the principal personnel, the firm's lay-out, function and its range of products. A receptionist must be fairly familiar with all the firm's activities as she must know who may deputise for an absent member of staff.

An organization chart (see page 76) may well be kept in a prominent position in the reception area. By reference to this the receptionist may at once, locate the person required. This, of course, is only necessary in large organizations with many personnel. In a smaller firm the receptionist will, no doubt, get to know the members of staff personally and will be familiar with their range of responsibilities and working habits.

Protocol

Protocol is another name for business etiquette and it means that there is a right way and a wrong way to do things. In every organization there is some protocol. For instance it is protocol to ask your immediate superior if your lunch hour might be changed in order that you might keep an important appointment. He or she would be very offended if you 'went over their head' to the top management.

There is a chain of command which starts with the Managing Director and finishes with the most junior member of the firm. It is usually 'frowned upon' if anyone steps out of the chain of command. No member of staff likes to find their own special responsibilities have been taken over by a colleague. It is very important, therefore, that the receptionist knows *who* is responsible *to whom* and *for what*. She must be careful to give each member of staff the respect which he or she considers necessary and, more importantly, information necessary for that person to carry out special duties in an efficient manner.

It is, of course, reasonable to expect a receptionist to act on her own initiative and she would be unwise to let 'protocol' hamper her when she makes a sensible judgement in the absence of the responsible member of staff.

Awkward callers and situations

A receptionist will find that she has to cope with numerous problems in the course of her normal working day. Bearing in mind the policy of her organization she should use her own common sense and initiative in dealing with any awkward situations. Situations may arise for which there has been no precedent and the receptionist may need all her tact and diplomacy in dealing with these. Basically, she must protect her employer from any sort of 'nuisance' but ensure that she gives no offence to callers in the process. The trained receptionist will need to learn how to deal with numerous difficult situations and this is best accomplished by the provision of practical situations and opportunities for role play within the framework of the course.

Problems

1 Sometimes a receptionist has to cope with an 'emergency' when an irate customer or client arrives at reception demanding to see a particular member of staff. Irate customers need to be attended to promptly otherwise they become increasingly angry. Such visitors must always be given immediate and courteous attention. These people should be seen as soon as possible by a member of the organization who is qualified to deal with them and capable of coping with their problems. If there is an unavoidable delay the receptionist may offer coffee and attempt to soothe the angry caller. At no time must she allow herself to be drawn into an argument but must parry all angry remarks with patient courtesy.

2 If a traffic warden came to the reception desk to say that the firm's van was double parked and causing an obstruction then the receptionist should apologise and assure the traffic warden that it would be moved at once. She must locate the driver of the van and ask him to move it immediately.

3 The receptionist, however, should act in a different fashion if the parking problem had been caused by a very important visitor to the firm. A very angry traffic warden needs immediate attention but the VIP is engaged in delicate negotiations with the management and it would be out of the question to ring through and ask for the car to be moved. Under these circumstances the receptionist should

a) contact the meeting,

b) ask for a written message to be discreetly handed to the VIP explaining the circumstances and suggesting that the car keys are given to the waiting messenger,

c) move the car herself (if a driver), or

d) if unable to drive, or unable to leave the reception desk, get a driver to move the car,

d) ensure that the VIP knows where the car is now parked when the keys are returned.

4 If a person arrives for a lunch appointment with an executive only to find that he has disappeared, and no one knows quite where, then the receptionist has quite a problem on her hands. While attempts are being made to trace the missing member of staff, his deputy (or someone capable of deputising for him) will be informed of the problem and may well decide to take the caller to

lunch himself. The caller should be told that the missing member of staff has been unavoidably detained. Apologies should be made and the caller should be assured that the missing executive will arrive as soon as he is able to do so. The caller would feel insulted, quite justifiably, if he thought that he was unimportant and had been overlooked.

Loyalty

A receptionist must be loyal to her firm and its personnel. She is her firm's representative and as such should endeavour to project her organization in the best possible light. For example, a visitor who called at 2.00 pm to know if Mr Good was available would receive an extremely poor impression if the receptionist replied: 'Mr Good – huh – you'll be lucky, he never comes back from his lunch until three o'clock. If I were you I'd come back then.'

Or when she is asked 'How are things?' the receptionist should never make remarks such as 'Oh slow – the time drags in this place! I'll be glad when it's five o'clock.' Or 'This is a mad house, nobody ever tells me anything and I'm expected to be in six places at once.' It is better for the receptionist to reply to questions such as these with brief answers such as 'Oh very good thank you,' or 'Keeping busy you know!'

Discretion

No receptionist should divulge information about her firm's affairs, even to the most inquisitive visitors. She should be discreet about all matters connected with her organization and its personnel. She is in a privileged position and should return her employer's trust in her.

A doctor's receptionist, for example, is in a very special situation. He or she is in a position to know the most intimate details of patients and their affairs. A receptionist who indulges in gossip, and who divulges confidential information either to satisfy personal feelings of importance or through indiscretion will do his or her employer and clients great harm.

A receptionist who is tactful, loyal and discreet, who is able to refuse people's requests without giving offence and use diplomacy, initiative and common sense will be a great help to her employer and enable her organization to function more smoothly and efficiently.

Questions

1. What information should a reception register contain?
2. Why is a business card useful to a receptionist?
3. What information does an organization chart give?
4. When a caller arrives without an appointment what should the receptionist's first task be?
5. What is tact? Why should a receptionist take special care to be tactful?
6. What type of person should a receptionist be?
7. Give the rules that should be employed when performing introductions.
8. Why is it necessary for a receptionist to have a thorough knowledge of her organization?
9. What is discretion and why is it essential that a receptionist be discreet?

Assignment 2

The following callers were received in your firm on Tuesday, 21 October.

1. Three young women called for an interview with the Personnel Officer, Mr Ron James. He was interviewing candidates for a vacancy in the Accounts department as follows:
   a) Miss Jane Bright of 14 Acacia Avenue, whose appointment was at 1015;
   b) Miss Amanda May of The Gables, Straws Lane, her appointment was at 1045 and
   c) Miss Joanna Pearce of 119 Rider Road, at 1115.
2. A salesman called at 1030 with no appointment. He wished to see the Purchasing Manager Mr Sanders. Mr Sanders was too busy to see him so the sales rep decided to write for an appointment to see Mr Sanders. The salesman's name was Mr Tom Hayes and his firm was Jenkins and Jones Ltd.
3. Mr L Champion from Yardley and Yardley, Solicitors, called to see Mr Dudley, the Company Secretary, by appointment. He arrived at 1115.
4. Mr L Blenkinsop of Allied Industries called to see Mr Evans, the Production Manager, his appointment was at 1130.
5. Miss Jones from the auditing firm Clarke and Webb called at 1145 to see the firm's accountant (Mr Lucas) by appointment.
6. Mr J Friar of Excel Office Supplies called to see Mr Sanders. His appointment was for 1200.
7. Mr Appleby of Reproductions Ltd called to see Mr Sanders at 1200. He had no appointment and left without making one for a future date.
8. Mr R Johnson called, by appointment, at 1230. He had an appointment with the Office Manager to give an estimate for decorating the main office.
9. An ex-employee, Mr Peter Spragge, called without appointment. He wanted to see Mr James of the Personnel Department. He waited for an hour and finally went in to see Mr James at 1230.
10. Mr F Hartwell called to see Mr Harris by appointment at 1230. Mr Hartwell's address is 224 Freedom Fields, Plymouth.

Draw up a reception register and, using the above date, fill in the information given in chronological order.

3 The reception area

Reception is usually situated near the main entrance of the building. Whether it be a smart hotel's foyer or a small cubby hole in a draughty hallway, part of the receptionist's duty will be to make it as attractive and as welcoming as possible.

People come to reception to get help, to find someone, to ask questions, to leave articles and to make appointments. A reception area that is bright, clean, tidy and attractive is really a very welcome sight to many callers, particularly if they have travelled some distance to reach the organization.

Reception should never have a 'cluttered' look about it. The receptionist should ensure that no personal articles are left lying about in full view of visitors. Handbags, gloves, and bits of shopping should be kept well out of sight either in a desk drawer or in shelves underneath the reception counter. It may be necessary for the receptionist to leave her coat and other outdoor wear in reception but these should be hung discreetly upon a peg in the background and not thrown across a chair or over a desk.

The reception area must be kept tidy at all times. Visitors will be in and out, leaving magazines and brochures strewn around and filling the ashtrays and waste-paper baskets. The receptionist must, quietly and unobtrusively, empty the ash trays (ensuring that all cigarette ends are out) and waste-paper baskets as often as is necessary. She should pick up discarded magazines and tidy the tables on which they are kept. The top of the reception counter must be kept reasonably free of articles so that visitors may place packages on it, write at it, lean over it and even empty the contents of their pockets or handbags on it!

The reception area is often comfortably furnished with arm chairs and low tables, carpets and a pleasant decor. The large multi-national companies are aware of the importance of first impressions and will spend many thousands of pounds in fitting out a sumptuous reception area. At the other end of the scale is the purely utilitarian area of the small country doctor who may have just a hatchway where his receptionist, nurse, dispenser checks the appointments off in her appointment's book and bids the prospective patient to be seated.

Most reception areas fall somewhere between the two and ALL of them will benefit from a vase or two of tastefully arranged flowers in their season, or pot plants and evergreens in winter. Brochures, trade magazines and periodicals are useful. Wallcharts, plans and drawings placed on the walls may be of great interest as well as helping to publicize the firm's products.

It is a good idea to have a visitors' coat stand. The circular type is ideal as it stands neatly out of the way in a corner. Those with space for umbrellas and walking sticks are useful but the receptionist should make sure that the visitors have all their belongings when they leave. Brief cases and handbags are seldom overlooked but umbrellas and walking sticks are a different matter!

A special cupboard may be used for lost property. A tag must be affixed to each article saying where and when it was found. A Lost Property Book must also be kept which lists the article found, the name of the finder, the place it was found and its present whereabouts. If the name of the owner is known, then he or she should be informed in writing that the property is in reception awaiting collection. When claiming lost property the claimant should be asked to describe the property, identify themselves and sign for the article. Valuable property must be taken to the police station and handed over. The police will need to know all the details of the item(s) found including the name of the finder. Lost property usually becomes the property of the finder if it is not claimed within six months.

Date	Where Found	Article and Description	Name of Finder	Action Taken
12 Nov	Left on reception counter	Black briefcase leather with gold clasp. Locked, no means of easy identification.	Miss R Jones	Taken to lost property cupboard
19 Nov	Found on coffee table in Reception	Pair yellow suede gloves. Slightly worn on RH palm. No identification	Miss R Jones	Taken to lost property cupboard
23 Nov	Found in lift	Wallet. Brown pigskin. £38.87 in cash. Credit card, signed L.M. Brinn. (Not known)	Mr S Wilkes	Taken to police station. Receipt attached

Figure 6   Entries in a lost property book

The receptionist must be aware of the need for security and for the secure storage of confidential documents and valuables. Most filing cabinets will lock and the receptionist must ensure that when the reception is unattended the cabinets *are* locked. It is, however, often a rule in organizations that there must be someone in attendance at the reception desk at all times. Some organizations keep petty cash in reception; this should not be kept in a box unless it is securely locked. The box should be placed in a locked drawer. For large amounts of money and for valuables, a safe may be provided. Very often the receptionist will know the combination but only when another member of staff is present will she be allowed to open the safe. Sometimes one member of staff knows half the combination and the receptionist knows the other half. This means that there will always be two staff members present each time the safe is opened. If reception is part of a large hotel complex then there might well be a special strong room for guests' jewellery and valuables.

Theft is a hazard faced by most firms and the receptionist may be responsible for closing and locking all windows and doors at the end of the working day.

In some organizations all staff are provided with lapel badges and staff identity cards. The identity cards are usually a photograph of the holder, complete with name and address, designation and signature. These are very useful in large organizations where staff are employed in positions of trust and responsibility and where leakages of confidential information would be serious for the organization.

A modern problem is that of bomb scares and it is quite common practice for visitors to submit to an inspection of their baggage. Some organizations do not allow cameras or holdalls inside their premises and these items are normally left with the receptionist who must, of course, be responsible for their safe-keeping.

Several amenities may be available in reception.

1 A pay phone   A receptionist may be asked on occasion if a visitor might use the phone. This is frequently inconvenient and so the management might consider the installation of a pay phone for the use of their clients. Pay phones may be wall-mounted or portable and a range of attractive signs are available to draw attention to their existence.

2 A coffee vending machine   In busy places, such as hospitals, individual attention is impossible and so a coffee machine is a very welcome item.

3 Literature for sale   In hotels and some large organizations there are revolving racks of guide books or leaflets of general interest. Visitors make their choice and pay at reception.

4 Tanks of tropical fish   These are sometimes maintained in the reception area and are attractive and colourful. Many people find them fascinating to watch and an enforced wait may thus prove to be less irksome.

Questions

1. Why do people come to the reception office?
2. Give three ways in which a receptionist can make a reception area look welcoming.
3. Give a simple set of procedures for dealing with lost property.
4. Why are wall charts of interest to visitors?
5. Name three amenities which may be provided in the reception area for the convenience of visitors.
6. The need for security in reception is obvious. State the ways in which **a)** documents and **b)** valuables may be stored safely.

Assignment 3

1. Make a list of accessories that you would like to see in a reception area.
2. Describe your idea of a reception area using the following words and phrases:

A vending machine
Lost property cupboard
Calendar
Magazines and journals
Clock
Pay phone
Company literature
Ash trays and waste paper baskets
Flowers and plants
Tropical fish tank
Carpets and curtains
Wall charts
A visitors' coat rack
Arm chairs
Low tables.

4 Business organizations

Receptionists will be employed by many types of organization but all are concerned with the following:

Management
Administration
Finance
Buying
Selling
Production of goods and/or services
Personnel

The work of each organization is divided into different departments, although in small organizations various duties may be carried out by just one or two individuals.

Management

The management of large firms is in the hands of the Board of Directors which is elected by the shareholders. The Board of Directors has special responsibilities towards the organization, the customers, the shareholders and the employees.

There are two types of director – executive and non-executive.

Executive directors work on a full-time basis as salaried members of staff and are well informed

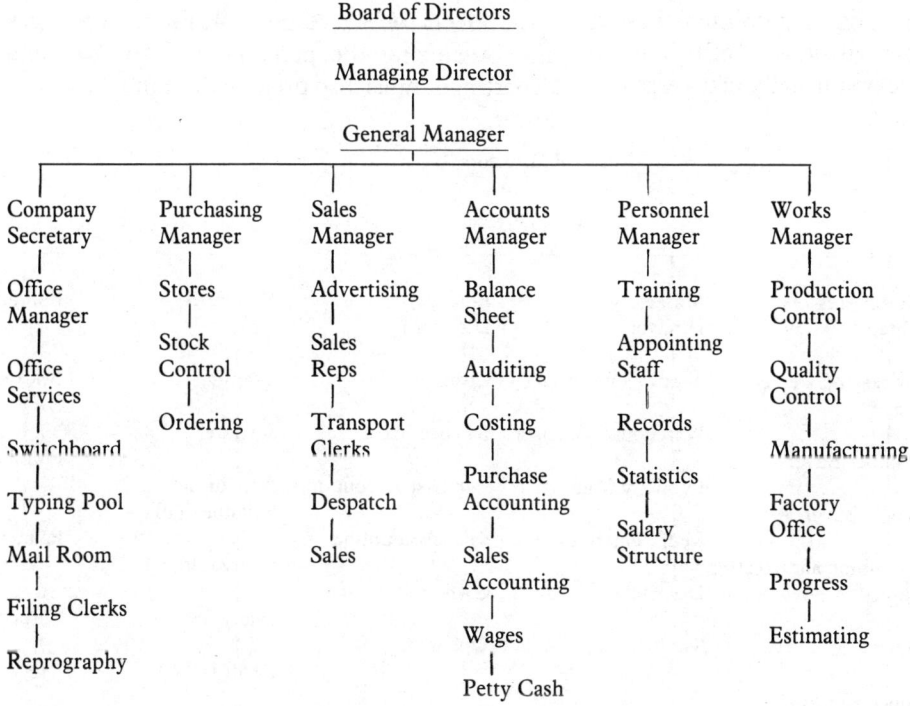

Figure 7   Organization chart of a medium sized manufacturing company

about the day-to-day departmental activities; they are available for discussion and consultation.

Part-time or non-executive directors are usually elected to the Board for their specialisation and expertise. They may be professional persons such as lawyers, architects or civil engineers.

A company will only be as efficient as its Board of Directors and a Board is only as good as its Managing Director. The Managing Director is the chief executive of the business, he or she formulates the policy and implements the Board's decisions. Together with the Company Secretary he or she forms the link between the Board and the executive of the organization.

Administration department

The Company Secretary holds one of the most important jobs in an organization. He or she is usually an Executive Director and is responsible for the following:

1 Keeping a register of shareholders;
2 Making statutory returns to the Registrar of Companies;
3 Organizing meetings between the Directors and the Shareholders;
4 Administration of the organization.

An Office Manager is often appointed to assist the Company Secretary with general office administration and he or she will usually take responsibility for the following:

1 Copy, audio and shorthand typists;
2 Office systems;
3 Reprography;
4 Filing;
5 The mail room;
6 Reception and the switchboard.

He or she must ensure that the work of all sections is properly co-ordinated, produced on time and that the administrative services are meeting the needs of other departments.

Finance department

This department is usually split into three main sections and is the responsibility of the Accounts Director.

Cost accounting is organized by the Cost Accountant who monitors budget expenditure so that the organization stays within the limits of its proposed expenditure.

Finance accounting is the responsibility of the Financial Accountant who is responsible for the purchase and sales accounting, (sending out bills to the organization's customers and paying the bills of the organization's suppliers.) The Financial Accountant must try to maintain a healthy cash flow.

The Chief Cashier is responsible for paying wages and organizing the petty cash. The Accounts department must also prepare the annual Balance Sheet.

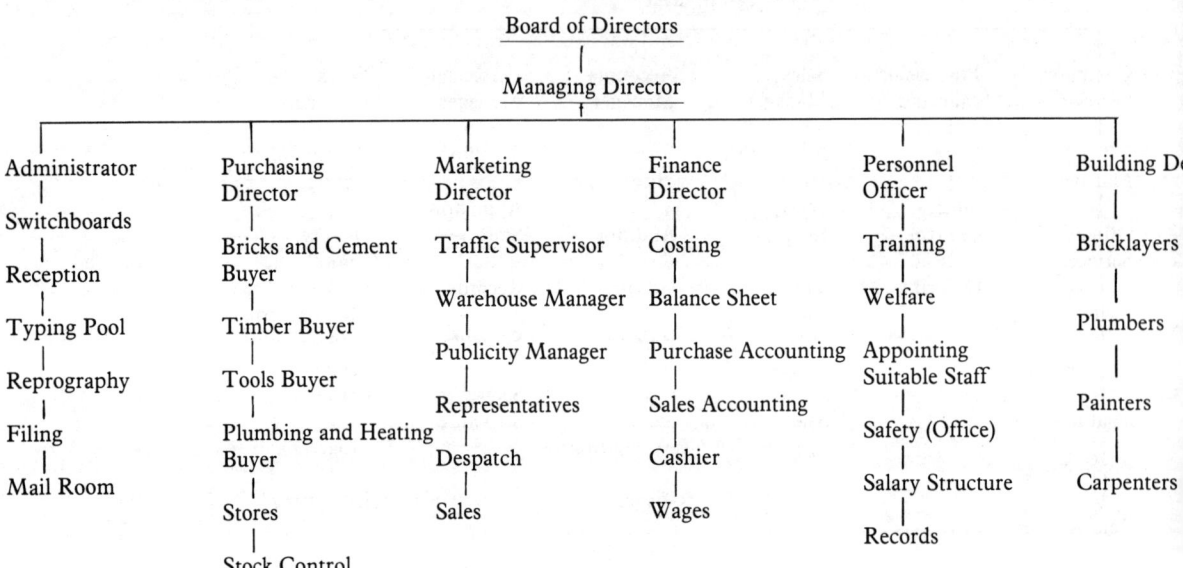

Figure 8   Organization chart of a wholesale builders

Purchasing department

Purchasing is the responsibility of the Purchasing Manager who will deal with all the buying requirements of the organization. These requirements will vary from raw materials to consumable office supplies.

The Purchasing Manager will collate all the information from other departments about items to be bought and buy as much as possible in bulk. Bulk buying is more economical as large discounts may be obtained. Information about sources of supply is built up over a period of time and it is part of the Purchasing Manager's job to attend trade fairs and exhibitions to ensure that suppliers are still quoting competitive prices. In addition the Purchasing Manager takes responsibility for the following:

1 Recording goods received;
2 Certifying purchase accounts for payment;
3 Maintaining stores and warehousing;
4 Maintaining an efficient system of stock control.

Marketing

This department is responsible for the marketing of goods or services produced by the organization. The Marketing Director attempts to discover what consumers need so that it can be manufactured, advertised and sold. Sections within the Marketing department include the following:

1 Market research;
2 Publicity;
3 A well-trained sales force;
4 Credit control;
5 After-sales service;
6 Export sales, documentation and knowledge of procedures;
7 Packing;
8 Transport.

Personnel

The Personnel Officer is responsible for the staffing of the organization. His/her duties include the following:

1 The selection and appointment of suitable staff;
2 The dismissal of unsuitable staff;
3 The wage and salary structure for all personnel;
4 The education and training of staff;
5 Statistics regarding sickness, accidents, staff turnover and holiday rotas;
6 Staff records;
7 Staff welfare;
8 Arbitration with the unions and with management;
9 Meeting the statutory requirements when employing and dismissing staff.

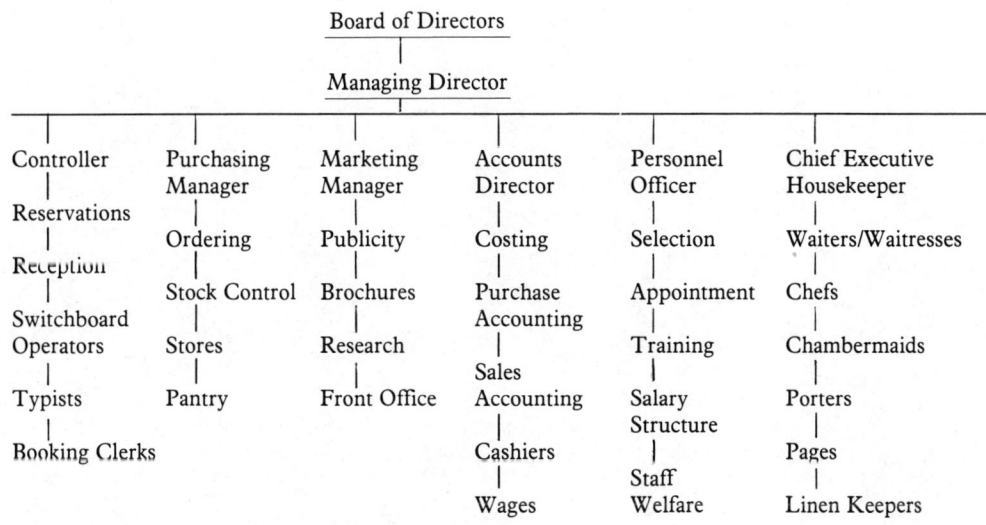

Figure 9 Organization chart of a typical hotel

Production

Production in a medium-sized manufacturing company is usually the responsibility of the Production Manager.

He or she liaises with the plant engineer who maintains the factory at an efficient level. He or she services, repairs and maintains the machines. The production controller makes certain that the production process runs smoothly by ensuring that the raw materials are readily available and that there are no bottlenecks due to faulty equipment and to poor workmanship.

The quality controller is responsible, through the Production Manager, for ensuring that all the goods produced are free from defects.

Part 2
Sources of information

5 Reference books

The receptionist will be asked numerous questions by all kinds of people. The senior members of the firm may ask such questions as:
'How do I address an archbishop?'
'How much is it to send an airmail letter to Zambia?'
'Who is the Prime Minister of Sweden?'
'What currency do they have in Paraguay?'
'What is the population of Aberdeen?'
And visitors may ask such questions as:
'What time is the next train to Cardiff?'
'Where can I get an interpreter?'
'Could you tell me if the Reverend Beamish is still the vicar of St Helens?'

A receptionist may be very efficient and intelligent but it is hardly likely that she will know the answers to such diverse questions. She *must* know, however, where to find the answers to these questions so that she can give the correct information to the people who need to know. All receptionists need to keep reference books in the reception area particularly the books that are in general and constant use. Telephone Directories list subscribers within the local telephone area in strict alphabetical order of the subscriber's surname. Where confusion might arise over indexing, a cross reference is made. For example, when looking up Social Security, Department of, the receptionist will find that the telephone directory will show, by the use of a cross reference, that it is indexed under Health and Social Security, Department of.

Apart from the list of subscribers the following information is available:

1 Inland call charges;
2 International call charges;
3 How to dial emergency services;
4 A list of all recorded telephone services and their numbers;
5 A description of up-to-date telephone equipment;
6 A comprehensive list of all telephone services;
7 Information on the telex service, facsimile transmission, datel, confravision.

The classified telephone directory, popularly known as Yellow Pages is listed according to occupation or institution. This is very useful to the receptionist when she needs to contact an individual or company to perform a specific service. Very often when a member of staff needs a photographer or a plumber he or she knows no one engaged in photography or plumbing – it is easy to locate someone by using the classified directory. The classified directory also carries advertisements.

A good dictionary is essential for a receptionist. Apart from the meaning of words, it gives the spelling and the pronunciation. There are also lists of abbreviations and derivations. Supplements on foreign words now being included in the general English vocabulary are often included in the standard dictionary. *Roget's Thesaurus of English Words and Phrases*, in which words are grouped according to their meaning, may be a complementary text for the receptionist as will *Fowler's Modern English Usage* which deals with awkward points of grammar.

The Post Office Guide gives a summary of all principal postal services, general postal rates and regulations both for inland and overseas mail. It also contains information on custom controls and currency. All overseas countries are listed alphabetically and regulations and rates for each country are given – under the heading of that country which is listed in strict alphabetical order. There is a section on telecommunication regulations and charges which includes the telephone, telegrams, facsimile transmission, confravision and the telex. Again, information is given for inland and overseas telecommunications.

AA and RAC (Automobile Association and Royal Automobile Club) books, which are issued for motorists who are members of these two organizations, list the towns of Great Britain in alphabetical order. Information is set out on their population, market day, early closing day, the distance of the town from London and other nearby towns. Hotels in the town are listed and rated according to their facilities available. This rating takes the form of stars – a five star hotel is recognised throughout the country as a very good hotel indeed. Garages in the vicinity are also listed together with the facilities that they offer to the motorist. A comprehensive set of road maps, distances in miles between the major United Kingdom towns, ferry services and hovercraft services are also given.

In addition to these general reference books the receptionist could find other books useful. An atlas or gazetteer will help the receptionist to discover the whereabouts of towns and countries abroad. She will find this particularly helpful if her firm is engaged in exporting goods when she will need to place frequent overseas phone calls and send letters and parcels abroad. ABC travel books which give timetables for air, sea, coach and rail, ferry and hovercraft sailings are also extremely useful. Visitors often ask the times of trains or ferry sailings and the receptionist might find great difficulty in obtaining information via the telephone as these lines are usually very busy.

The most comprehensive reference book in the English language is *Whitaker's Almanack*. It gives complete information on the following:

1 The United Kingdom, its past and present Kings and Queens, the Royal family, Cabinet Ministers and all Members of Parliament. The Peerage, the Law Courts, the Church of England, the Bank of England and the Privy Council.
2 Information on the United Kingdom and the British Commonwealth – the principle cities and their populations, area, governments, agriculture, and vegetation. The governments of the USA, information on the EEC and the United Nations. World statistics on housing, crime, agriculture, railways, fishing, manufacturing, population and mining.
3 British and foreign embassies, rulers of foreign countries, flags and emblems, monetary systems.
4 Nobel prize-winners, sport, music, films, drama and literature.
5 Trade unions, weights and measures, the calendar year.

A selection of books which give the correct forms of address and information on precedence, qualifications, honours and other information on notable people are available. The best known reference for this type of information is *Who's Who*. There is also *Who was Who* for information on past notabilities and *International Who's Who* for the prominent people who reside abroad. *Black's Titles and Forms of Address* is also a useful reference book as it will give information on precedence and the way that one should address persons of rank.

There are also specialised reference books which contain very detailed information on various sections of the community, mainly by occupation. It would not really be necessary for the receptionist to keep these books in her office but she must be aware of the information that they contain and be prepared to go to the local reference library to find the answer if need arises.

1 *Directory of Directors* appears each year and gives an up-to-date list of directors and their companies.
2 *Kelly's Directory of Manufacturers and Merchants* gives a list of Suppliers and Manufacturers arranged in alphabetical order of the goods or services that they supply.
3 *Stock Exchange Year Book* gives complete details regarding companies, securities, shares and investments.
4 *The Law List* is a reference book which gives information on various magistrates, law courts, judges, solicitors and barristers.
5 *The Navy, Army and Airforce Lists* give details of all service officers, their careers and their appointments. These books also give other information regarding the organization of the armed services.
6 *The Medical Directory* gives comprehensive

lists of all qualified medical practitioners.

7 *The Dental Register* lists all qualified dentists.

8 *Crockford's Clerical Directory* gives details of all Church of England clergymen, their livings and their parishes.

9 *The Municipal Year Book* will give comprehensive information about all the local authorities in England and Wales. The council officers, population and area is given for each local authority.

10 *Willing's Press Guide* contains information about newspapers and periodicals published in Britain.

We can see then that a comprehensive store of information on every subject and for every profession is available to anyone who knows where to look.

Questions

The Statesman's Year Book
1. How many teacher-training colleges are there in Britain?
2. Where is Pennsylvania – what is its capital city?
3. What is the population of Manchester?
4. Who is the Prime Minister of Iran?
5. How many states are there in the United States of America?
6. What number of MPs go to make up the House of Commons?

Whitaker's Almanack
1. What is the flag of Greece?
2. What is the main agriculture in Spain?
3. Who is the Queen's private secretary?
4. *When* did Princess Anne marry? *Who* did Princess Anne marry?
5. What is the population of Algeria?
6. Who won the Nobel Peace prize last year?

Who's Who
1. Who did Sir Laurence Olivier first marry?
2. When was Margaret Thatcher born?
3. What was the name of Dennis Healey's father?
4. Who did John Silkin marry?
5. What date did Sir Harold Macmillan become the Prime Minister?
6. Where did Lord Snowdon go to school?

The Post Office Guide
1. What is the fixed charge for sending an international telegram to Paris?
2. What is the cost, per minute, of a telephone call to Austria?
3. Is it possible to send a child's toy to Malta?
4. How much time are you allowed for 5p when phoning Holland?
5. What does the Post Office designate as a trap packet?
6. What is the highest compensation one can arrange when sending valuables through the post?

The Classified Telephone Directory
1. What number would you ring for information about a boarding kennel for dogs?
2. The number of an office supplies wholesaler.
3. The name and the address of the nearest taxi firm.
4. The name and the address of the nearest plumber.
5. The phone number of the local library.
6. The phone number of the local police station.

The Telephone Directory
1. Find the number to dial for the AA Road Report.
2. Find the number to dial for the latest weather news.
3. Find the most expensive time of day to make a telephone call.
4. Find the number of the local comprehensive school.
5. Find the number of the local Social Security office.
6. Find the number for the latest financial news.

The Local Code Book
1. Find the code for Oxford.
2. Find the code for York.
3. Find the code for Glasgow.
4. Find the code for Llandudno.
5. Find the code for Birmingham.
6. Find the code for Edinburgh.

The AA/RAC books
1. Discover the early closing day in Oxford.
2. Which is market day in Abingdon?
3. Find the two best hotels in Winchester.
4. Discover the population of Southampton.
5. Find the best garages in Newbury.
6. Find the distance between Penzance and London.

Miscellaneous
1. Look in the *Medical Directory* and find out where Dr B J Foster did his medical training and where he is now in practice.
2. Find out the name of the Commandant of Sandhurst College. Find also, his regiment and his rank.
3. Look in *Willings Press Guide* and discover when *The Daily Telegraph* was first published and how much it then cost.
4. Find out when I M F Hine esq first qualified as a solicitor and where he now has a practice.
5. Find out the time of the overnight train from Penzance to Paddington during the month of June. Is there a sleeper car?
6. Look in the *Municipal Year Book* and find the name of the person responsible for education in Dorset and the population of that county.

Assignment 4

Three executives of your firm are to travel from their areas to Paris for a meeting with their French counterparts. They will travel on the Tuesday of the first week in October and wish to complete their journeys without an overnight stay. The meeting will be 1400–1600 hours.

a) Mr A J Brown, London Area Sales Manager, wishes to use British Airways.

b) Mr H McIntosh, Glasgow Area Sales Manager will travel as he usually does, by British Caledonian from Abbotsinch to Gatwick and then on to Paris.

c) Mr C Stevens, Birmingham Area Sales Manager, wishes to use British Midland Airway flights.

The receptionist is required to type or write out three itinerary cards, one for each person covering their forward and return flights and showing airports/terminals to be used. Staple each card on A4 paper so that they can be read.

Answer the following questions.

1. Give the telephone number in Paris for the Europcar enquiry desk at the appropriate airport and ring to have a Europcar waiting to travel to his appointment.
2. How does Paris time relate to GMT?
3. How could you find out the current exchange rate for the franc?
4. How can telephone calls to France be made?
5. Can photo telegrams be sent to Paris?
6. List the reference books you have used for this assignment.

6 Teletext and Viewdata

The receptionist should be aware of the most modern methods of reference by way of the television screen and the telephone.

Teletext

During all normal television broadcasting hours 'newspapers' are available on all television channels. The BBC call their teletext service *Ceefax* (See facts). The Ceefax sub-editors type pages on the monitor screens visual display unit. They take their material from the visual newsroom services – agencies, teleprinters, BBC news services, ITV and the radio and make it into material suitable for Ceefax's format. It is then fed into a computer which stores the pages and transmits each one at 25 second intervals.

The Ceefax users tap in on push-button controls the number of pages that are required. When the first page appears on the screen it is held there until another page is ordered. Whichever page the Ceefax users wish to see will come up in anything from 0–25 seconds and will be shown on the television screen. As with a conventional newspaper, Ceefax's main interest is news, but it has sections on the weather, entertainment, consumer matters, finance and sport. The great advantage of Ceefax over the news services that are provided by other media is that it is instantaneous. The Budget and General Elections can be covered; all the news may be presented instantly. The news editor may shuffle pages into any order that he or she thinks fit. Maps and diagrams using different colours may be used. These can be superimposed on the normal pictures with great clarity. Particular pages may be ordered in advance so that as soon as the result of, say, the third race at Ascot is announced it will appear on the screen.

Oracle, ITV's rival to the BBC's Ceefax, is a very good medium for advertisers to bring up-to-date information on sales and services.

To obtain Teletext a special recorder must be added to a television receiver, once this has been done the transmission is free. Some of the larger hotels are now installing this facility for their guests.

Viewdata

The new telecommunication system providing thousands of pages of 'on screen' information sent via ordinary telephone lines is Telecom's Viewdata service called *Prestel*. It will eventually be in a position to connect every business, Government agency and household in Great Britain to memory banks of computers all over the world.

This vast amount of knowledge will be supplied in the same way as Teletext, through the medium of a slightly modified television set. Prestel, however, is also connected to a telephone line and a small plastic box which looks a little like a calculator. This is the keypad.

Because Prestel is linked to a computer there is almost no limit to the amount of information it can store and to which the receptionist may have access. At the present time there are more than 150 organizations providing information to the Prestel computer and between them they have booked over 180 000 pages of information which is available to Prestel users via their television screen. Although this is an impressive amount of knowledge it is expected that the system will be quite capable of providing over one million separate pages of information in the near future. Most importantly, this information will be regularly up-dated so that a change in the weather forecast for example, or even the latest cricket score, is fed into the system almost as soon as it happens.

The receptionist who is employed in almost any business offering goods or services will find that Prestel has a special significance. From market intelligence to airline schedules, from manufacturing and service industry guides to foreign exchange rates there are literally thousands of Prestel pages with an immediate and very practical relevance to the successful and efficient running of the businesses of today, both large and small.

Prestel is expected to become international which will give access to information stored on computers throughout the world, and all of this will be available within seconds. It is also expected that in the near future Prestel will start a shopping-off-the-screen facility. It will be possible to place orders via Prestel for goods or services advertised on the screen and even pay for them by transmitting a credit card number.

The main difference between Teletext and Viewdata is that Viewdata is a two-way system using telephone lines. This gives users the opportunity to conduct a conversation with the Prestel computer and possibly in the future, other Prestel users. Ceefax and Oracle are one-way broadcast services which are sent out on the same transmission as conventional television programmes. In practice they are like television newspapers supplying constantly up-dated information which will be, predominantly, news. Although Prestel supplies news, it is also an enormous library of reference and other information to which a subscriber can refer at any time.

Teletext and Viewdata

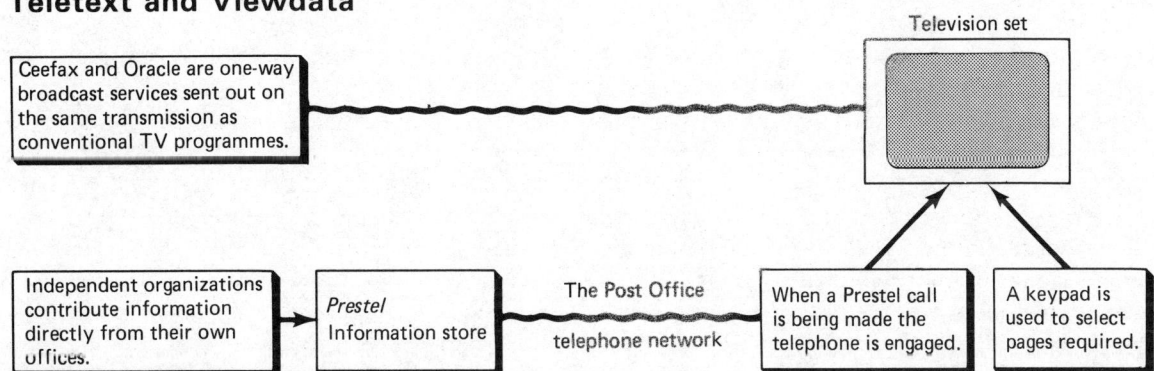

Figure 10   Teletext and Viewdata

Questions

1. What is the main difference between Teletext and Viewdata?
2. What is meant by 'Prestel is a two-way communication service'?
3. What other great advantage has Viewdata over Teletext?
4. Give four reasons for the growing importance of the Viewdata service to the business person.
5. What significance will Viewdata have for the receptionist who has access to this reference material?
6. What is the name given to the Teletext service provided by
    a) the BBC and
    b) ITV?
7. How does the BBC sub-editor obtain up-to-the-minute information to display on the teletext service?
8. Describe briefly how Prestel works.

Assignment 5

Assume that you are employed as the receptionist of a firm and that you have been asked to plan a visit for an important speaker.
Name of speaker Sir Martin Ryle
Date of visit 25th May 198

1. Find out what the initials after his name stand for.
2. Find out brief details about his life (eg date of birth, education, marriage, interests) so that your employer will know something about him when he gives his vote of thanks after the speech.
3. He is travelling down to Cornwall on the day before he is due to speak and will be staying in Newquay for the night. Find the name of a suitable hotel where he can stay for the night and its address and telephone number. Calculate the approximate cost of one night at this hotel in a single room with breakfast.
4. He is travelling back to London in the afternoon, having given his speech in the morning. He will be travelling by train from Truro and is to be driven by taxi to the station. Find the name of a suitable taxi firm and its telephone number.
5. He must be back in London by 2200 hours. Find the time of a suitable train from Truro that will get him there in time and give the time of the train's departure and arrival.
6. Make a list of the books of reference and other sources of reference from which you have obtained the information together with the answers to the questions.

7 Other sources of reference

Apart from reference books a great many receptionists will require really up-to-date and current information. Teletext and Viewdata are obvious sources of this type of information but apart from these there are many other sources to which the receptionist can refer.

All Government departments are willing to help the public when queries arise. A telephone call to the relevant department will often produce the required information. For example, from the Customs and Excise the receptionist may obtain the following information:

1 The regulations and rate governing the payment of Value Added Tax;
2 Information on excise duties which are payable to the Treasury;
3 Information on customs duties which are now payable to the European Economic Community;
4 Information on imports and exports about licenses and prohibitions;
5 Information on harbours throughout the United Kingdom – their dues and the regulations.

Embassies and High Commissions are in existence to represent their countries. A great deal of very detailed information may be obtained from these sources. For example; the Brazilian Embassy would be in a position to give information about:

1 The currency and the rate of exchange against the pound;
2 Centres of population;
3 The main industries;
4 Agriculture and vegetation;
5 The Government and its officials.

Trade delegations may be contacted on matters of trade, imports, exports and import tariffs. For instance, a Japanese delegation visiting this country would be in a position to answer the following queries.

1 Are there any restrictions on importing porcelain into Japan?
2 Are import licences necessary?
3 Who is the person to approach about obtaining specialist information about these matters?

The *Daily Telegraph* has an information service and will answer queries that are sent in by telephone or letter. They are in a position to supply many facts and, if unable to produce the required information, will often be able to suggest other sources which might be able to give the answer.

Professional institutes such as the Institute of Banking are concerned with the work of their profession, its standards and its regulations. Any queries regarding banking might well be answered quickly and efficiently as they are more than willing to help the public in their own particular field.

Travel agents and tourist offices will provide general information about travel, rates of exchange and may even know where interpreters may be hired.

The Post Office is a mine of information. Numerous leaflets are obtainable at all post offices with detailed information on many diverse subjects such as packing a parcel or obtaining free dentures! Apart from these leaflets it is possible to obtain information regarding mail handling and mail regulations, driving licence information, regulations concerning premium bonds, and so on.

The telephone also gives a great deal of

information with its numerous recorded services. It is possible to obtain up-to-date information on the weather, the time, the financial news, road conditions, the latest test match score etc.

Job Centres and Youth Employment Centres will give current information on job opportunities and employment.

For up-to-date travel information there are a variety of organizations which the receptionist might try. The more obvious ones such as coach stations, rail stations and airports are often very busy and the receptionist might find that she will waste a great deal of time dialling numbers that seem to be permanently engaged. Travel agents are very helpful but it is a good idea for the receptionist to provide herself with up-to-date rail and coach timetables. The Automobile Association (AA) and the Royal Automobile Club (RAC) are always very helpful and if the enquirer is a member of the organization they will be willing to plan a route for a special journey by road.

Trade journals are specialist magazines or periodicals for a particular trade or profession. Useful information may be obtained from magazines such as *The Bookseller*, *The Hotelier*, *The Draper* etc. Addresses of trade associations can be found in Trade Directories which are available in public libraries.

The receptionist should not neglect, however, the most obvious source of information and that is the Public Relations Department of a firm, Public Relations Departments are only too pleased to answer any queries about their products or services.

The reference section of the local library will contain all the reference books that a receptionist will need and the reference librarian is always helpful and willing to give any aid and advice about sources of information.

Questions

1. Where would one go to obtain information on VAT?
2. What sort of information would one obtain from foreign embassies and High Commissions?
3. Where would one go to get information on
   a) banking and
   b) advertising?
4. Which newspapers give an information service?
5. Give five items of information that one may obtain over the post office counter.
6. What sort of information is obtainable from trade delegations?
7. The Citizens' Advice Bureau gives information on various topics. What are they?
8. Travel agents are useful sources of information. Name three items on travel which they are often able to supply.

Assignment 6

An overseas customer (Australian) is going to visit your firm (Oxford Enterprises Ltd) for one week during the summer; his wife and his twin son and daughter, aged 16, will accompany him. Your firm has branch shops at Abingdon, Newbury, Witney, Woodstock, Bicester, Banbury, Thame and Aylesbury. The customer will accompany your employer for four days of the week on visits to the branches (two per day).

a) Draw a sketch map.
b) Type a rota of towns.

Show the proposed visits and the mileages involved by car to and from Oxford. They will visit a town in the morning, lunch there, go to the next nearest town in the afternoon and then back to Oxford.

c) Suggest one or two local attractions or activities at or fairly near each town on the rota which might interest his family during the half day while he is busy. Any details that you can give regarding times of opening eg stately homes, charges etc will be helpful to your employer when he writes to the customer regarding arrangements for the visit. Assume that the family will use the car each half day.

d) Plan activity/entertainment for the spare day and one evening in Oxford. This activity can be separate, if you wish,
(i) for the customer and his wife,
(ii) for the twins.

Give some estimate of the likely cost of (i) and (ii).

Part 3
Office routines

8 Appointments book and diaries

Usually a private secretary will keep an appointments book for her own employer and will inform the receptionist each morning of the list of appointments for her own particular employer.

Thursday 20th March		MR OLIVER
1000	Visit from Swedish Delegation	Head Office Conference Room
1145	Tour of Boat Show with Swedish Delegation	
1300	Lunch at Greenoble Hotel	Greenoble Hotel
1500	Bank Manager Barclays – High Street	Mr Oliver's Office
1630	Meeting of Advertising Staff	Board Room

Figure 11 An appointments diary

The receptionist may, therefore, find that she has six or seven different lists of appointments which will be confusing for her to follow. It is her responsibility to correlate them so that she has a list of the visitors who are expected to call at the organization on any specific day. This list should be set out in chronological order, which is the order in which they will arrive. She should also ensure that she has information about any executive who will be absent for all, or part of, the day.

If the receptionist has to make appointments for the various executives she should always remember to write clearly, printing all names and initials. All essential information should be included. It is impossible to remember why a person required an appointment unless it is written down at the time. It would be embarrassing if a member of staff queried an appointment with, say, Mr H Thomas for 1500 hours on 6th April and asks what Mr Thomas wants, only to discover that the reason for making the appointment has been forgotten by the receptionist.

The receptionist should know where to contact the potential visitor in case the arrangements have to be changed.

When making an appointment for any senior member of staff from the receptionist's own organization it is a good idea to make the appointment initially by telephone, thus getting a prompt decision. However, written confirmation of the telephone conversation should be made as quickly as possible, usually the same day. A carbon copy should be kept of this letter as this will give a permanent written record for the receptionist's files.

When making important appointments for an executive always try to follow it with routine or less important appointments. It is then not so bad if a distinguished visitor overstays his time allocation. It is good practice to allow a little time between appointments. They must not be made so closely together that the executive feels eternally under pressure. He or she must be given a little time to relax, to consult a relevant file or even to have a cup of coffee.

A receptionist may also be required to type appointment cards for various personnel who have to be away from the office for a whole day. This should not be too large and should accompany any documents that the member of staff is taking.

Time	Visitor	Business	Staff Member
0900	MR H BLISSETT	Demonstration of new copier	MR WATTS Office Manager (Room 21)
0930	MISS L FAWCETT	Probation Officer re H Coombes	MR JOHNSON (Personnel Department)
1000	SWEDISH TRADE DELEGATION	Goodwill Mission	MR OLIVER (Conference Room)
1100	MR M PURDIE	Discussion of new insurance clause	MR ROYSTON Company Secretary (Room 16)
1100	Coffee for Swedish Trade Delegation		
1115	MISS M BRINN	New Sprinkler system for building	MR WATTS (Room 21)
1115	MR L FORBES	Representative from Carrs Ltd	MR GOLIGHTLY (Room 38)
1130	MR M MARTIN	Applicant for Clerical vacancy	MR JOHNSON (Personnel Office)
1200	MR S FRY	Auditors re books	MR ROYSTON Accounts (Room 19)
1400	MR L SIMPKINS	Representative from F H Miles	MR GOLIGHTLY (Room 38)
1430	MR O MARGETTS	Solicitor	MR ROYSTON (Room 19)
1500	MR A DEAKIN	Bank Manager	MR OLIVER (Room 219)
1530	MRS L MOBBS	Applicant for Clerical vacancy	MR JOHNSON (Personnel Department)
1630	Advertising Staff Meeting		Board Room

Figure 12   A receptionist's appointments book

Appointments Card

MR. OLIVER

1000 — Swedish Trade Delegation
       Conference Room
1100 — Coffee
1145 — Tour of Boat Show
       (Tickets Enclosed)
1300 — Lunch booked for nine
       at Greenoble Hotel
1430 — See Trade Delegation off
       at Central Station
1500 — Mr. A. Deakin
       Room 219
1630 — Advertising Staff Meeting
       Board Room

Figure 13   An appointments card

Questions

1. One of the executives has asked you to cancel all his appointments for next week. How would you deal with this task?
2. Why is it necessary for the receptionist to correlate all the appointments for each member of staff?
3. Why should important appointments be followed with routine appointments and duties?
4. Why should carbon copies be made when letters of written confirmation of appointments are sent out?
5. Why does a receptionist need to know where to contact a potential visitor?
6. Explain the use of a receptionist appointment's book and give a typical page with six entries.

Assignment 7

One of the firm's executives, Mr O Haines, writes down the following appointments for next Monday.

1. Mr H Weldon – during the morning
2. Mr L Bray, auditor, morning or afternoon
3. Mr J Tompkins, solicitor, afternoon
4. Mr L Everett, accountant, afternoon
5. Mrs S Swinderby – Personnel Director. Lunch.

Mr H Weldon's office is 15 miles from the organization. The appointment with Mr Tompkins is very important. His office is about 20 minutes drive away from the organization. Mr L Bray's office is about five minutes' walk from Mr Tompkins and Mr Everett's office is about ten minutes by car from Mr Haines's own office. Mrs S Swinderby is a colleague of Mr Haines and will need to be met and taken to the Hotel Splendide for lunch.

Write the appointments for the day for Mr Haines, giving suitable times for the appointments and planning his day with the least amount of travel.

9 Visual aids

Information is more easily and far more rapidly understood when it is presented in pictorial form. This information may be displayed so that facts, figures and trends may be seen or understood at a glance. The receptionist may need to display information of this type in the reception office and will occasionally be called upon to prepare the charts and graphs.

Line graphs may be employed to show almost any type of information particularly for a company selling goods. Police use them to show crime rates, hospitals use them to show the temperature of patients, statisticians use them to show death rates. They are very widely used for differing types of information.

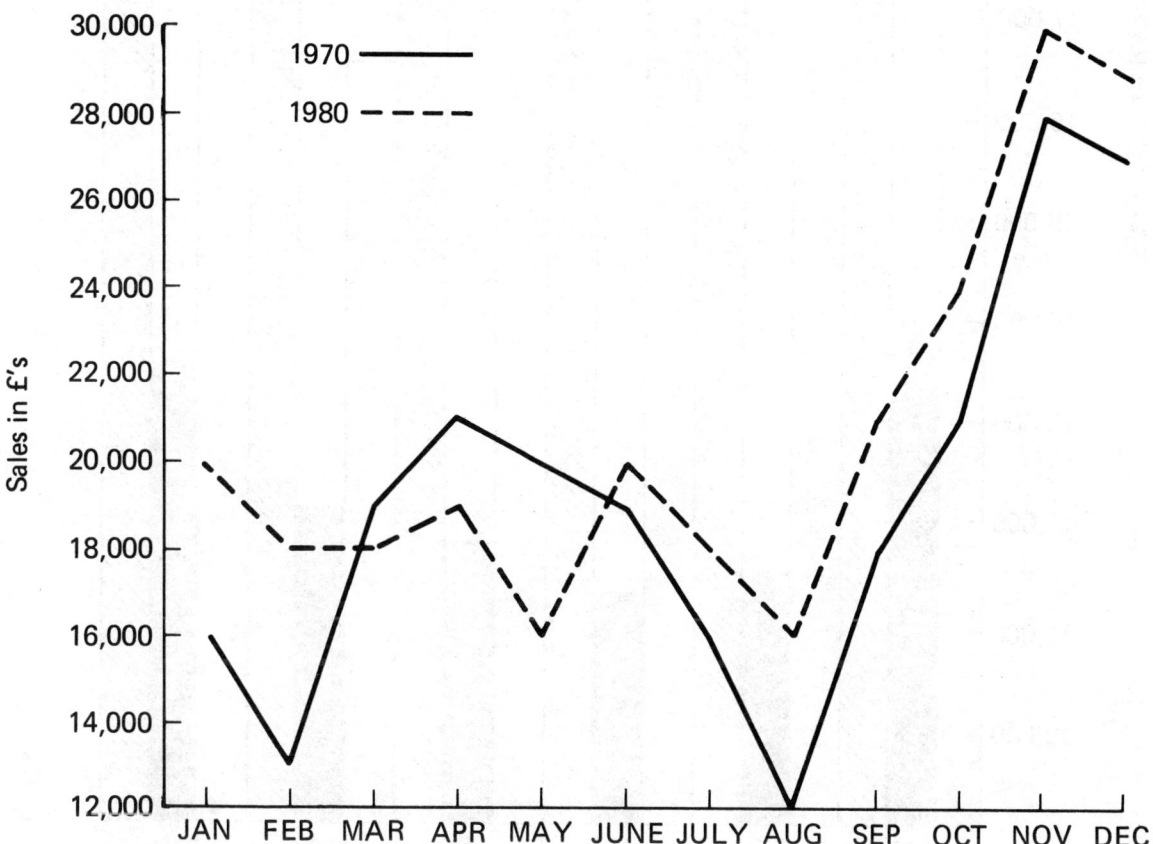

Figure 14   A line graph

Bar charts are very similar to line graphs but individual bars rather than a continuous line are used to display information. By this method of display, comparisons between one product and another are extremely obvious and provide visual impact. It is important that a clear key is provided.

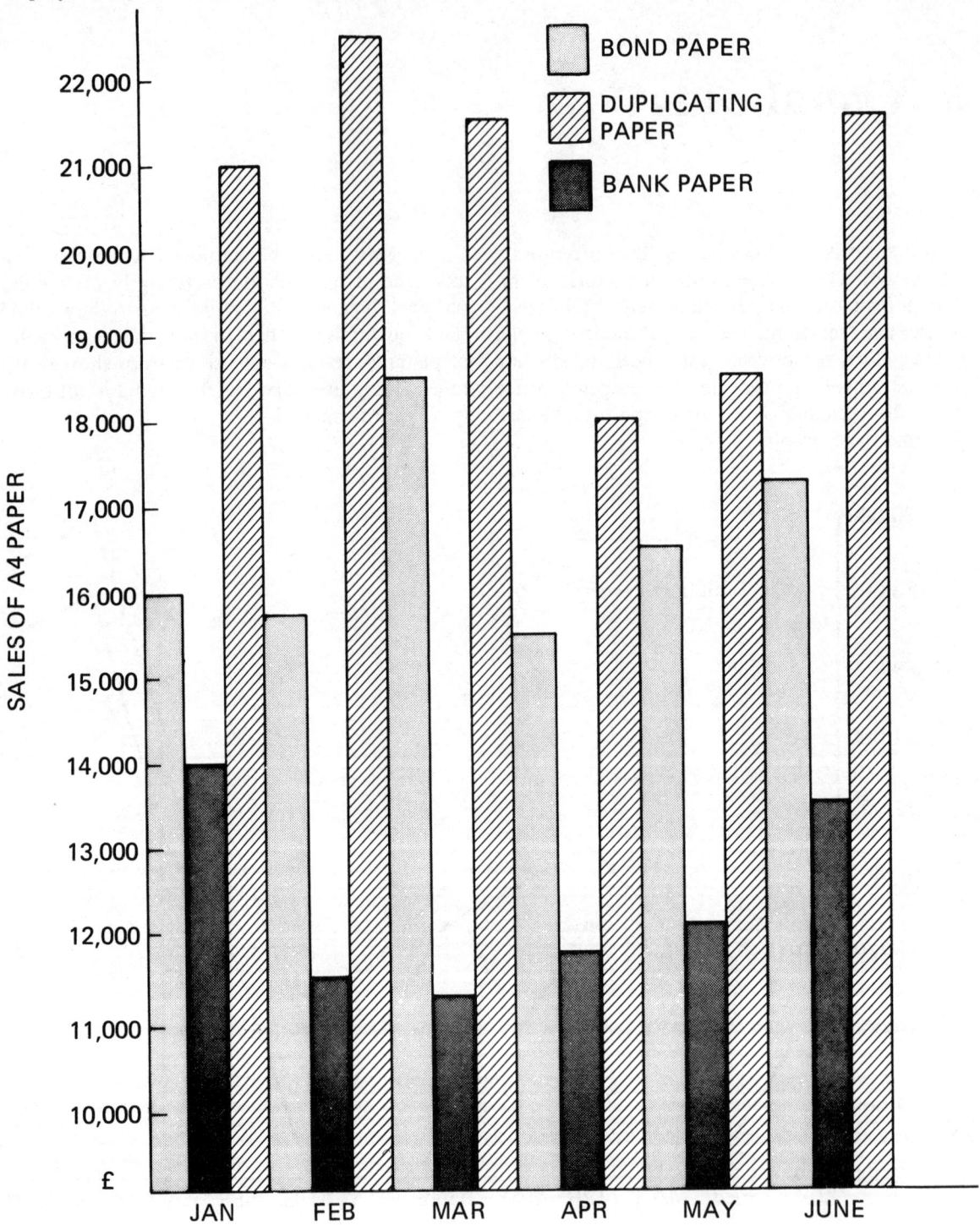

Figure 15   A bar chart

Pie charts are a very common method of displaying information when the information to be displayed shows proportions of a total. Each section of the circle shows the proportion of the total amount involved.

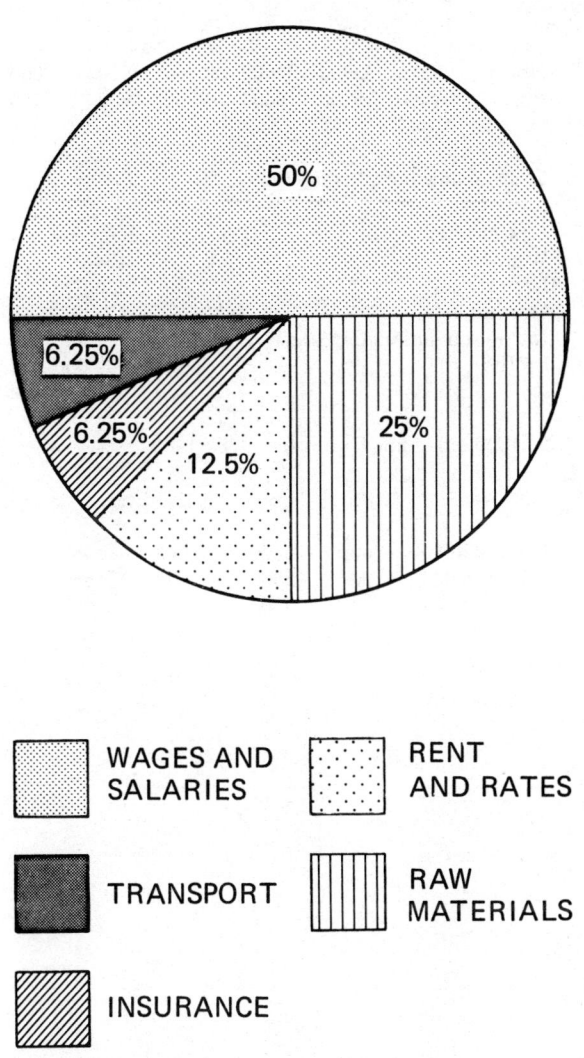

Figure 16 A pie chart

Questions

1. Look at the bar chart in Figure 15 and answer the following questions.
   a) In which month was the most duplicating paper sold?
   b) In which month was the least bank paper sold?
   c) Show the bar chart as a line graph.
2. Show the line graph in Figure 14 as a bar chart.
3. Draw a pie chart showing the information given below
   The expenses of a general store
Wages	50%	Heating	6¼%
Food	25%	Linen, cutlery, china	6¼%
Advertising	12½%		
4. Describe the various ways in which facts and figures may be displayed.
5. What are the advantages of recording information in graphic or chart form?

Assignment 8

You are employed by Williams and Sons, domestic electrical appliance manufacturers. A board meeting is to be held at the end of the week.

You are asked to present the following information in both tabular and graphical form. Examine the following data and produce graphs and charts that show the facts in the best way.

1. Sales figures for Williams and Sons for 1980

	Jan	Feb	March	April	May	June
Home	19200	27600	20500	18600	19800	22600
Export	14900	15850	16100	15900	12430	1980

	July	Aug	Sept	Oct	Nov	Dec
Home	25800	32900	34900	36800	28200	23000
Export	27750	16100	16000	18500	19000	17100

2. Breakdown of costs for 1980

Raw materials	£200 000
Wages	124 000
Investments	26 000
Overheads	51 000
Interest on outstanding loans	12 000
Profits	90 000

3. Production line figures for 1978–1980

1975	Irons	Toasters	Chimes	Hairdryers	Foodmixers
1978	9200	4200	5600	3800	4600
1979	11 100	6100	5800	4300	6800
1980	12 400	5800	5100	7200	9600

10 Reminder systems

No matter how efficient a receptionist may be it is impossible for her to remember everything that she is told. She must, therefore, have an efficient reminder system.

One type of reminder system is a desk diary and this would be quite suitable in a small organization. Some firms, however, have many future appointments and documents needing further action. In this case a desk diary would be inadequate and a 'tickler' system should be inaugurated.

A tickler system is kept in a card index drawer. Appointments and reminders are written or typed upon postcards and placed in the card index in chronological order. A guide card is prepared for each month of the year and also a series of guide cards numbered 1–31. These numbered cards are guides for the current month. The tickler file is arranged so that the current month is in the front of the file with cards for 1–31 inserted in numerical order. The following months are placed behind the current month in correct order.

If an executive asks the receptionist to make an appointment or remind him of a letter to be written, an anniversary to be remembered or even a visit to the dentist to be noted, then the receptionist should write out a card for the tickler file showing the date, the item, the time and the place. The cards should then be filed immediately behind the guide cards bearing the date on which the action should be taken.

At the end of the current month the next month is brought to the front of the drawer, the 31 numbered cards are placed in numerical order within that month and all the reminders already prepared should be filed in position.

A hotel receptionist may need wall charts and visual planners. Hotels often have very complex planning requirements; it is important for the receptionist to be able to see at a glance precisely what rooms in an hotel are available and when they are vacant. A large chart showing dates and rooms should be displayed in the reception area. When answering telephone enquiries about bookings or availability of rooms the hotel receptionist will need to be able to answer many enquiries promptly and make bookings without any delay.

Figure 17   Visual control board

Several kinds of visual control boards are available.

1 Plastic self-adhesive boards contain a smooth, transparent plastic covering. The tabs are small pieces of plastic which are manufactured in various sizes and colours. These contain enough static electricity to remain in place when lightly pressed onto the board.

2 A magnetic system uses strips which can be magnetically attached to a visual control board. It is easy to detach and move the strips. This, also, is particularly useful for showing hotel reservations and vacancies.

There are numerous types of visual control boards but the plastic and magnetic boards are probably better for the rapid change of information required by hotel receptionists. Another type of visual control board which would be useful to a receptionist is the card rack type. This consists of a framework of channels into which the cards may be fitted. The cards might have the names of senior staff written upon them and the rack could show the layout of the organization so that it would be possible to see the whereabouts of personnel at any given time.

Questions

1. Describe a tickler file.
2. Of what use is a visual planner to a hotel receptionist?
3. Give two other uses for a visual planner in a reception office.
4. Give three types of visual control board.
5. Design a visual control board showing the whereabouts of all the teachers on your college course during one week.
6. Design a visual planner so that the Sales Manager will be able to see exactly where each member of his sales force is located. The sales force consists of ten representatives who each cover six specific areas. They are located in each area for a week at a time. Use your initiative concerning the names of the representatives and the areas they cover.

11 Flower arrangement

The reception area, as already stated, is usually welcoming and attractive. Flowers are often in evidence as they give beauty and colour to their surroundings. Very often a certain amount of money is set aside each week for the purchase of fresh flowers and it is usually the duty of the receptionist to buy and arrange the flowers.

Choosing flowers

It is better on the whole, for reasons of economy, to buy flowers in season. Long stemmed roses in December may look beautiful but they are going to be very expensive to buy. For the same reason, flowers such as lilies and carnations should be purchased sparingly. These flowers are expensive as they are rarer and more difficult to grow. Late winter is an exception, there are very few flowers available and potted plants are a good buy at this time of the year as these may always be re-sited in various offices once the spring blooms are starting to appear again.

Conditioning

Once the flowers have been purchased they should have their stems cut diagonally so that more of the stem's surface is exposed to the water. Tough, fibrous stems such as chrysanthemums, need to have the skin scraped off below the water-line and the stems roughly broken. Leaves rot quickly when under water so all foliage that will be below the water-line must be removed. Excess foliage above the water-line should also be removed. If there are too many leaves on one stalk then the blossoms may be starved of water and they will then wilt and die. Once the flowers have been put in water they should be kept in a position away from direct sunlight and away from draughts. The evaporation of moisture caused by too much heat or by draughts will cause the flowers to die prematurely.

Containers

When thinking about the size and the shape of containers it is well for the receptionist to think about the position that they will eventually occupy. For reception desks and small tables, low bowls are most generally useful as these do not seriously interfere with the line of vision. The receptionist may have an area where very tall flowers, autumn foliage or branches of spring blossom will look attractive. This will usually be in some corner and for this she will need a tall, heavy vase which holds plenty of water and will not be inclined to topple over. In addition to the containers the receptionist will need a sharp knife and some blocks of plastic foam. The foam anchors the flowers in place and is essential when the flower arrangements are placed in low bowls.

Arrangements

There are two types of arrangement – line and mass.

For line arrangements the receptionist should select the longest blooms and complete the highest line first. Before cutting the stems of the flowers she should hold them away from her and let her eye judge the right height and angle.

Mass arrangements are easier as the receptionist may start at any point but she must check it from all angles from which it will be seen as it must have balance and depth.

There are various books which the receptionist may borrow or buy which will teach her a great deal about flower arranging and about the flowers themselves. There are also short courses on this subject at colleges and the receptionist might be able to take advantage of this. A beautiful floral arrangement will enhance any reception area and will provide a welcoming touch for visitors to the organization.

Questions

1. Why is it better to buy flowers in season?
2. How should the receptionist condition flowers after she buys them?
3. Why should flowers be placed away from sunlight and direct draughts?
4. Explain why the selection of the right container is so important.
5. Name the two main types of flower arrangement.
6. Why should the receptionist learn something of the art of flower arranging?

12 Entertaining

The receptionist may not be called upon to entertain visitors apart from offering coffee and biscuits to callers who are waiting to see a specific member of staff. Occasionally, however, the organization may have a cheese and wine party or a sherry party. This usually happens if the firm wishes to entertain some of its more important clients, or, if the firm is launching a new product or a new service.

When the firm launches a new product or service the member of staff responsible for public relations will invite members of the press, editors and writers of trade journals etc. It is on occasions such as these that the receptionist may be asked to provide refreshments. If the party is to be a large one then obviously the management will ask outside caterers to provide the food, drink and the service. When entertaining the receptionist should ensure that she knows the type and style of refreshment required by the management.

Cheese and wine

When arranging a cheese and wine party the receptionist should endeavour to gain some knowledge of different wines.

Table and beverage wines

There are so many classes of table wine that it would only be confusing to list them here in detail. The most common types are:
French White Bordeaux – Graves, Sauternes, Barsac etc.
French White Burgundy – Chablis, Hermitages etc.
French Red Claret and Burgundy – Beaujolais, Beaune, St Julien etc.
French Pink – Rosé
Italian Chianti – Red and White
Spanish and Portuguese Sauternes and Burgundies are cheaper imitations of some of those previously mentioned.

Sparkling wines

Sparkling wines include champagne. The name *Champagne* is jealously guarded. The district in which it is grown is very small and only wine produced within this district is entitled to be called champagne.

Fortified wines

These are wines where the fermentation has been checked at a certain stage by the addition of alcohol which fortifies or increases the alcoholic content. Sherry, Port, Madeira and Marsala are examples.

Sherry is a very confusing wine and the receptionist should spend a little time getting to know the main types. Sherry is a *blend* of wines of various years and styles. The variation of styles in sherries is so great that it is never safe for a receptionist to serve sherry unless she enquires of her visitors as to the type of sherry they would like. Usually she will just need to enquire whether 'dry' or 'sweet' sherry is preferred. There are two main types of sherry – fino and olorosa. The finos are pale and dry; olorosa is dark and sweet. There is a range of sherries between fino and olorosa which are the 'golden' sherries. These range from light to full rich, therefore a 'pale golden' would be dry, yet not as dry as a fino and a 'full golden' would be richer in colour and very much sweeter.

The receptionist should endeavour to store wine in a rack so that the cork is always in contact with the wine and does not dry out. The bottles should be kept still and out of draughts.

All white wines including champagne, should be served cold. Red wines, and fortified wines should be served at room temperature. The sweeter the wine the cooler it should be. Ice should never be placed in *any* wine. Champagne needs to be served very cold indeed and ice may be packed around it if the receptionist has access to a fair amount of ice. Storage in a refrigerator for a period of time is often an adequate substitute.

The cheese

The main hard cheeses are Cheddar, Cheshire, Caerphilly, Double Gloucester and Lancashire; semi-hard cheeses include Gruyère, Emmental and Parmesan; softer cheeses are Camembert, Brie and Petit Suisse varieties. Blue vein cheeses are popular and this variety includes Stilton, Wensleydale, Danish Blue and Gorgonzola. A variety from each type should be included so that guests may find their own particular favourite available. The cheese may be served with a variety of types of cracker and small dishes of nuts, crisps, stuffed olives and cocktail onions etc may also be served for guests to help themselves. Many different forms of cocktail specialities such as tiny cocktail sausages, small tinned prawns etc may be stuck on sticks and served with the cheeses.

When serving a group of visitors the receptionist must serve the most important guest first. If unsure of the relative importance of individuals then it is as well to serve the most elderly guest initially. When serving the wine the chief executive (or the member of staff who is playing host for hostess) should be served with a small amount of wine which he or she will probably wish to smell and taste, before it is served to his guests. After his or her approval, serving always from the right-hand side of each guest, the guest of honour (if there is one) should be served, the next person and so on around the room until the receptionist has served everyone.

Coffee

The receptionist will almost certainly be expected to produce coffee throughout the day. There are many types of coffee she may choose. Instant coffee, of course, is very much easier and very much more convenient to serve to visitors. However, ground coffee is considered by the majority to be very much more pleasant and the caller is likely to be more satisfied if handed a cup of freshly percolated coffee.

If the receptionist wishes to serve ground coffee she may buy it freshly ground and keep it in a sealed container until required. An electric coffee percolator may be purchased or the receptionist may employ the cona method of making coffee which consists of a small boiling ring and metal or glass percolators.

Generosity with coffee is a fairly inexpensive way of entertaining and this simple gesture will create a lasting impression of goodwill.

Questions

1. What are 'public relations'?
2. Name the three broad categories of wine.
3. What is fortified wine?
4. Explain the difference between 'sweet' and 'dry' sherry.
5. At what temperature should
   a) white wine and
   b) red wine be served?
6. How many types of hard cheese are there? Name them.
7. Who is usually served first at any social gathering?
8. Why is the host or hostess given wine before the guests are served?

13 Receiving parcels and messages

A receptionist, in addition to dealing with parcels through the mail, may also be expected to accept parcels delivered by rail and road transport.

All parcels so delivered are accompanied by a delivery or a consignment note which lists the number of parcels, the contents, reference number or marks and the name of the supplier. They should also show the order number of the ordering firm.

The receptionist should check the parcels very carefully and only sign for them if:
a) her firm has ordered the goods;
b) the parcels really do contain the goods listed on the note;
c) the quantity is correct;
d) the parcels are undamaged.

If a carrier arrives with goods and has no order number quoted on the delivery note then it would be as well for the receptionist to check with the Purchasing Department to ensure that the goods really have been ordered. Most firms will stipulate that no goods will be accepted unless their order number is quoted at the time of the delivery so the receptionist must *never* accept goods without checking upon this.

She must then verify that the parcels do, indeed, contain the correct goods. If they are securely wrapped then a corner of the wrapping

```
DELIVERY NOTE            BRAY WHITEHEAD & CO LTD
                         PARK ROAD      OXFORD

NUMBER  334381           TELEPHONE 0865 41418
                         TELEX     OX1K 36366
DATE:   20th March 1981

TO    STIMPSONS (OXFORD) LTD    Please receive the following:-
      HIGH STREET
      OXFORD                    Your order  312466 refers.


      6 desks (oak, three drawer)   ref K6043




      Signature of receiver _____ Date _____
```

Figure 18 A delivery note

STIMPSONS (OXFORD) LTD HIGH STREET OXFORD				
GOODS RECEIVED NOTE NUMBER X856 DATE: 20th March 1981				
NO. ORDERED	NO. RECEIVED	NO. REJECTED		NO. ACCEPTED
6 Desks Ref.k6043	6	1 desk - Corner Damaged		5
Received by:-	H. Vinton Storeman	Date: 20th March 1981 Delivery note no. 334381		

Figure 19   A goods received note

must be broken so that the receptionist may discover the exact contents of the parcels.

The number of parcels must be counted and recounted to ensure that the correct number has been delivered. Any damages must be noted and the receptionist may be required by her firm not to accept damaged goods.

After receiving the parcels the receptionist will make out a Goods Received Note so that the Accounts Department will know precisely what they must pay for. They will need to ask the supplying firm for a credit note should there be any shortages or any damages.

Messages

Some organizations employ special messengers to deliver messages, letters, notes, memoranda, telegrams etc. Messengers are also employed to collect internal and external mail from the various offices throughout the day. In a hotel, pageboys deliver messages to guests in restaurants and lounges, call guests and visitors to the telephone and to meet friends and relations who might be enquiring for them at the reception desk.

To ....
Date ....

WHILE YOU WERE OUT

Mr. ....
of. ....
Phone No. ....

Telephoned		Please call him	
Called to see you		Will call again	
Wants to see you		Urgent	

MESSAGE
....
....
....
....
....

PD7   Operator ....

Figure 20   A message pad

If a verbal message is left for a member of staff or a guest then the receptionist should record it on a special message form.

She will either call a messenger (if that is the practice within her organization) or a junior to take the message to the designated member of staff with-

49

out delay. If that member of staff is absent from the office then the junior should inform the receptionist so she may verify that the message has not been overlooked by the member of staff.

Messengers may also be responsible for taking parcels and delivering letters to other organizations. Receptionists should ensure that:
- **a)** the name of the addressee and the address is clearly written;
- **b)** the messenger is given clear directions as to route (using a street directory if necessary);
- **c)** is reimbursed for all bus or taxi fares from the petty cash.

Questions

1. Why do most accidents occur?
2. Give five problem areas where falls might occur.
3. Why should gangways and all corridors be kept clear?
4. Fire precautions should be known to all personnel – give the receptionist's duties in case of fire.
5. List the duties of the employer regarding the prevention of accidents.
6. What is the duty of employees with reference to the Safety at Work Act?
7. What purpose does the Accident book serve?
8. How long must the accident book be kept after the last entry?

Assignment 9

You have just started work as a receptionist. On the first morning your boss explains to you the importance of safety. He gives you a copy of 'Spot the hazards' picture.

1. Make a list of what you consider to be hazards and dangers in the picture. Note all the points as briefly as possible and number them separately. You should produce at least twenty items on your list.
2. An accident happens to one of the male office workers in the picture. The nurse in the company's First Aid room decides that the injured office worker should go to hospital because of what she regards as the serious nature of the injury. Complete the accident report form on pages 55 and 56.
3. According to the company's Accident Report Book you discovered that last year the company's accidents were as follows:

Major Accidents	7 head injuries, 12 eye injuries, 9 broken limbs, 24 injuries to the back, 12 removals to hospital;
Minor Accidents	95 cuts, 40 bruises, 60 torn clothing, 50 falls, 1 removal to hospital.

Construct a bar chart to illustrate this information.

Figure 21 Spot the hazards

Electrical cables, switches and plugs must be carefully maintained and not left to fall into disrepair. Plugs must be earthed and no sockets should be overloaded, electric machines such as duplicators should have a 'fail-safe' switch and electric fires must be guarded.

The receptionist may do a tremendous amount to make her organization a safer place in which to work by her own vigilance and by warning the management of potential danger spots. She should also have some knowledge of the Health and Safety at Work Act 1974.

'It is the duty of the employer to consult representatives of the employees with a view to the making and maintenance of arrangements which will enable him and his employees to co-operate effectively in promoting and developing the health and safety at work of the employees and in making sure that the measures are effective'....

AND

'Every employee has a duty while at work:

a) to take reasonable care for the health and safety of himself – and of other persons who may be affected by his acts or omissions at work.
b) as regards any duty or requirement imposed by his employer or any other person or under any of the relevant statutory provisions to co-operate with him so far as is necessary to enable that duty or requirement to be performed or complied with'

In other words it is the employer's duty to provide and maintain a safe environment in which employees may work. It is the duty of the employees to take reasonable safety precautions and to co-operate with the management in making the organization's premises a safer and healthier place in which to work.

The accident book

The accident book must be kept in every organization which employs more than ten persons. This book may be obtained from Her Majesty's Stationery Office (HMSO) and the receptionist should record all details of accidents which have occured to employees whilst they were engaged in carrying out their normal daily duties.

The following instructions appear on the front cover of the Accident book:

'The purpose of this Accident Book, which is the duty of the occupier to keep under the provision of Regulation 23 of the Social Security (Claims and Payments) Regulations, is to assist an injured person in giving notice of accident to his employer as required by regulations made under Sec. 88 of the Social Security Act, 1975, and an entry in this book, if made as soon as practicable after the happening of the accident, will be sufficient notice of the accident for the purpose of that Act.

This accident book has to be kept at every factory, mine and quarry, and also at every other works or premises to which any of the provisions of the Factories Act, 1961, apply, and at any other premises on or about which ten or more persons insured under the Social Security Act are normally employed at the same time in connection with the employer's trade or business.

The book must be kept at such place as to be readily accessible at all reasonable times to any injured employee and any person *bona fide* acting on his behalf.

Particulars of an accident may be entered herein either by the injured person himself or by someone acting on his behalf.

The accident book when filled up should be preserved for a period of three years after the date of the last entry.

Note: Every employer is required to take reasonable steps to investigate the circumstances of every accident recorded herein and, if there appears to him to be any discrepancy between the circumstances found by him and the entry made, he is required to record the circumstances so found.'

Questions

1 What information should a delivery note contain?
2 Give the four most important points that should be looked for when a receptionist receives parcels.
3 Why should the receptionist check with the purchasing department if there is no order number on the delivery note?
4 What is the purpose of a credit note?
5 Why should the receptionist make out a copy of the goods received note and to whom should she send the copies?
6 How can a receptionist verify that a parcel contains the correct goods?
7 How can the receptionist ensure that important messages are not overlooked?
8 What are the duties of the messenger in a large organization?

14 Safety and fire precautions

Most people know that accidents in the home and at work are increasing yearly and yet there is very little awareness of this fact among the personnel in offices, hotels and shops.

The receptionist can do a great deal to minimize the risk of accidents. The genuine accident is really very rare; most result from oversight or carelessness. It will never be possible to eliminate accidents completely but if the receptionist takes accident prevention seriously and is aware of the possible hazards then she may help to make her organization a safer place in which to work.

Frayed carpets, torn or badly worn lino, projecting nails, loose floorboards and highly polished floors all bring about falls. Any danger spots such as these should be noted by the receptionist and reported to the management.

Visitors are always unaware of potential hazards such as an unexpected step up or down, swing doors that fly open violently and steep stairs. When a lift is installed in the building visitors should always be escorted to the required floor by a messenger or by the receptionist herself.

Deliveries of stationery and office requisites should not be left lying around the reception area to trap the visitor. These should be stacked neatly out of the way until a messenger or porter arrives to remove them. The porter or messenger should not be allowed to carry awkward or extremely heavy parcels as this in itself may bring about an accident.

The receptionist should always use a safe step ladder to reach high shelves. Heavy books, box files and ledgers that are balanced precariously on a shelf may fall at the slightest vibration so they need to be stored very securely. When filing cabinets are overloaded in the top drawers, or when more than one drawer is opened at a time then they may topple forward with very nasty consequences.

A great many mishaps are caused by 'bumping' into someone. Personnel become absorbed in a report or some important papers while walking across the reception area. They may push open glass doors without looking to see if someone is on the other side and a person struck by a glass door could suffer serious facial injuries. There is not really very much a receptionist can do here except to draw attention to such a situation by displaying a warning notice or special warning posters which may be obtained from the Royal Society for the Prevention of Accidents, the British Safety Council and such like organizations.

The receptionist should provide plenty of ash trays and pleasantly request all visitors to use them if they smoke. Cigarettes left smouldering on the edges of tables or window-sills are a fire hazard. The receptionist should not empty ash trays into a waste paper basket without ensuring that all cigarettes are thoroughly extinguished and wastepaper baskets should not be placed too near to an electric fire or other heating appliance.

Fire precautions should be known to all personnel. The receptionist should be aware of the positions of all the fire extinguishers and should know the drill for evacuating the premises in case of fire. She must also know how to prevent the rapid spread of the fire by closing windows and doors and unplugging all the electrical appliances. She should, personally, escort visitors to safety if possible. In a hotel, however, it would not be possible for the receptionist to make herself responsible for the visitors. The current fire precautions, however, ensure that fire escapes are provided and fire doors installed.

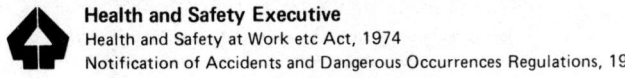

Health and Safety Executive
Health and Safety at Work etc Act, 1974
Notification of Accidents and Dangerous Occurrences Regulations, 1980

Report of an accident and/or dangerous occurrence and injuries sustained

Please read the notes on pages 1 and 2 before completing this form.

Part I Administrative

1 Person or organisation reporting the accident/ dangerous occurrence

Name _____

Address _____

_____

_____ Postcode _____

Nature of undertaking _____

Signature of person making this report _____

Date _____

Name *(block capitals)* _____

Position in organisation _____
(where applicable)
Tel no _____ Ext _____

2 Place of accident/dangerous occurrence if different from 1 (for construction sites give name of main contractor)

Name _____

Address _____

_____

_____ Postcode _____

Tel no _____ Ext _____

Name of site manager or other person in charge *(block capitals)* _____

Address *(if not as above)* _____

_____

_____ Postcode _____

Tel no _____ Ext _____

Part II General report of the incident

1 Date _____ 2 Time _____ *am/pm

3 Precise place, e.g. South Warehouse, No 2 Machine Shop, canteen kitchen

_____

4 Was there a dangerous occurrence as defined in the regulations? yes ☐ no ☐

If yes, state type _____

5 Number of (a) deaths _____ (b) major injuries _____

6 Give a full account of the accident/dangerous occurrence, explaining so far as possible how it happened and how those killed or hurt received their injuries. Give name and type of any plant, equipment, machinery or vehicle involved and note whether it was in motion.

F2508   *delete as appropriate   Part III — overleaf

Figure 22 An accident report form

55

Part III Details of injured/deceased person(s)

This part should be completed for each person for whom a direct report is required — those included at 5(a) and (b) of Part II (see notes). Space is provided for two persons; if more is needed attach further copies of the form as continuation sheets (number the cases consecutively).

(At questions 3, 4, 8 and 9 tick the appropriate box ☑)

Case number _____   Case number _____

1 Surname _____   1 Surname _____

2 Forename(s) _____   2 Forename(s) _____

3 Was he/she: 3 Was he/she:
   at work as an employee? ☐   at work as an employee? ☐

   at work self-employed? ☐   at work self-employed? ☐

   not at work, but injured as a result   not at work, but injured as a result
   of work activity? ☐   of work activity? ☐

4 Male ☐   Female ☐   4 Male ☐   Female ☐

5 Age last birthday _____   5 Age last birthday _____

6 Address _____   6 Address _____

_____ Postcode _____   _____ Postcode _____

7 Occupation *(for employees and self-employed persons only)* e.g. carpenter, electrician   7 Occupation *(for employees and self-employed persons only)* e.g. carpenter, electrician

8 Was the injury fatal?   yes ☐   no ☐   8 Was the injury fatal?   yes ☐   no ☐

9 Was he/she treated in hospital for more than 24 hours?   9 Was he/she treated in hospital for more than 24 hours?
   yes ☐   no ☐   yes ☐   no ☐

10 Nature and site of injury (e.g. compound fracture of left leg, loss of right eye, amputation of right hand)   10 Nature and site of injury (e.g. compound fracture of left leg, loss of right eye, amputation of right hand)

11 What was he/she doing at the time of the incident? If he/she fell, how far?   11 What was he/she doing at the time of the accident? If he/she fell, how far?

Signature _____   Date _____

Name *(block capitals)* _____

on behalf of (organisation) _____

20p net; 25 copies for £2.25 (exclusive of tax)
Printed in England for Her Majesty's Stationery Office by Trafford Press Ltd., Doncaster
Dd.022943 K2000 2/81 ISBN 0 11 883367 7

15 First aid

The Health and Safety at Work Act makes it obligatory for all organizations to have at least one member of staff with a knowledge of first aid. Because of the increasing number of accidents at work this is essential and the first aid officer carries a great responsibility.

A receptionist, being at the centre of activity, is in a very good position to render first aid and it is often an excellent idea for potential receptionists to take a course in first aid at the local St. John's Ambulance or First Aid establishments. Certificates are awarded to candidates who have attended a course of theoretical and practical work and who have passed a special examination which tests their knowledge.

This certificate is only valid for three years which ensures that the first aid officers are regularly examined and kept up-to-date in knowledge and skill.

First aid is the aid given in an emergency until *medical aid* can be obtained. Many people actually endanger the lives of the casualties through ignorance of the correct procedures. Basically it is the task of the first aid person to prevent a casualty from becoming worse before he receives medical attention, eg bleeding to death.

The initial action to be taken by the first aid person is to give confidence to the casualty. She or he will do this by being calm, talking and listening to the casualty and reassuring the person. She or he must always be gentle and careful in handling and move the injured person as little as possible. It is essential that she or he protects him or her from the cold with blankets but the body should not be heated with such things as hot-water bottles as this will draw blood from vital organs to the surface of the body.

Pain should be relieved as much as possible but it is often difficult to do this. If there is a suspicion of internal injuries nothing should be given to the casualty to eat or to drink as this may cause complications if an operation is needed on admittance to the hospital.

If breathing has stopped, or is failing, the casualty's air-passages should be cleared, (nose and mouth) and emergency mouth-to-mouth resuscitation should be started.

When a casualty has wounds with severe bleeding, the aim of the first aid person is to stop bleeding and obtain medical help urgently. The first aid person should know the pressure points – where a large artery may be compressed against a bone – to prevent the flow of blood beyond that point. Such pressure may be applied for up to fifteen minutes only, as bodily tissues are irreparably damaged when deprived of blood for longer than this period.

Wounds may be covered to prevent further infection and to absorb any discharge. The dressings should be sterile if possible and should act as a filter to further infection. Dressings also help blood to clot.

Before moving a casualty all suspected fractured parts should be supported by providing splints which are rigid and long enough to immobilise the joint above and below the fracture. Such things as walking sticks, umbrellas or even broom handles may be used as improvised splints.

Occasionally a first aid officer has to deal with an individual who has fainted. The patient should be laid flat with the legs raised slightly above the head level. The clothing around the neck and the waist should be loosened and the first aid person should ensure that the casualty can breathe freely.

Burns and scalds are extremely painful but some of the pain can be alleviated by immersing the burned area in cold water or by placing the burned area under slowly running water, the colder the better. This reduction of heat is essential, not only to lessen the pain but also to lessen the spread of heat in the affected area. All constricting clothing must be loosened and the casualty laid down. The burned area must be covered with a clean dressing to minimise the infection and no lotions, ointments or oil must be used. Small amounts of cold drinks should be given at frequent intervals to replace the fluid loss and so lessen shock. As with other casualties, reassurance is of enormous importance.

The first aid person will arrange for the casualty to be taken to the nearest hospital or to their home as quickly as possible. She or he should also summon a doctor in serious cases. When an ambulance is required she or he should send for it stating the exact place of the accident or emergency (with directions as to route if required) and some indication of the type and the seriousness of the emergency should be given.

The first aid officer should not allow spectators to crowd around the casualty as this may use up air and it will sometimes distress the patient.

A receptionist who has taken a first aid course will be invaluable to her organization. She will be much in demand for her knowledge and her expertise. Her self-confidence will grow as she deals with small everyday problems such as nose bleeds, splinters and sudden fainting spells. Hopefully, she may never be called upon to deal with an emergency or with an accident involving multiple casualties but should this happen, she may find that her prompt actions will prevent a serious and difficult situation from becoming a great deal worse.

Questions

1. Why is it essential that someone in an organization should have a knowledge of first aid?
2. What is first aid?
3. For how long is a First Aid Certificate valid?
4. Why is it important to reassure a casualty?
5. Why should the first aid person refrain from giving the casualty
    a) a hot water bottle?
    b) anything to eat or to drink?
6. Why should all wounds be covered?
7. What is mouth to mouth resuscitation?
8. a) What are pressure points?
    b) Why should they not be compressed for longer than fifteen minutes?

Part 4 Communications

16 Telephone services and their use in business

Not every firm has so many callers that the services of a full-time receptionist are required. Very often the receptionist will be required to act as a switchboard operator as well as a receptionist. She should, therefore, have a thorough knowledge of all telephone services and their use in the business world. She should also know the approximate and relative costs of making a telephone call. Where subscriber trunk dialling facilities are available, 'local' and trunk calls are charged in units of 3p–4p for periods of time depending on the chargeable distance of the call and the time of day as well as the day of the week. So a call made to another firm over 35 miles away on a weekday morning between 0900 and 1300 hours will cost £2.76 for ten minutes. It will be seen, therefore, that if calls are not strictly controlled the organization could spend a great deal of money.

STD (Subscriber Trunk Dialling)

By obtaining the correct code from the STD booklet, subscribers may dial to almost every place in Britain without having to ask the operator to connect the call.

IDD (International Direct Dialling)

International Direct Dialling works the same way as STD. A code is employed to connect callers with towns and cities in Europe. Canada, USA, South Africa, Australia and New Zealand, India and Japan are all reached by IDD. These services make it easy for the receptionist to dial direct to organizations in Britain and abroad. She must be aware of the international date-line and the time differences, however, as she (and the organization) would be extremely unpopular if she telephoned Australian contacts during her working day only to find that she had woken them at two o'clock in the morning their time.

The following services are very useful to the business person.

The time (speaking clock) By dialling the number the receptionist can discover the exact time correct to one twentieth of a second.

Business news The receptionist may call the *Financial Times Index* and *Business News Summary*. The Financial Times Industrial ordinary share index is updated seven times daily, Monday to Friday, along with a stockmarket report, company news and tomorrow's Business Diary. At weekends there is a summary of the past week's dealings on the Stock Exchange.

Motoring information The receptionist may be required to obtain information on motoring conditions. This is information supplied by the *Automobile Association* within 50 miles of each centre shown in the directory preface. This service is especially useful for members of staff who have to drive to meetings and appointments in other areas.

Weather Sometimes an executive wishes to know a weather forecast; weather information is supplied by the Meteorological Office in London.

Emergency services By dialling 999 the receptionist will be connected to the exchange operator at once. The operator will connect her to the required service. Emergency services are the Police, Fire-brigade, Ambulance, Coastguard and Lifeboat.

Advice of duration and charge It is necessary, on occasions, for organizations to know the exact cost of a specific call. The receptionist should ask the operator at the time of making the call to advise her of the duration of the call and its cost. A fee is payable in addition to the charge for the call.

Fixed time call If an executive has an important call that he or she must make, the receptionist may book in advance a fixed time call with the operator. This will be connected at or about the time specified. A series of daily fixed-time calls over consecutive days can also be arranged.

Alarm call A receptionist may arrange to be called at any time of the day if, for any reason, she needs to be reminded of an urgent appointment. She may also arrange for an executive to be called early in the morning if he or she needs to be awakened for an earlier than usual start to the day.

Personal calls If a receptionist is having difficulty in contacting a person in a hotel or a large firm she may book a personal call. A personal fee is payable as soon as the call is answered but the charge for the call does not begin until the person required can be brought to the telephone. Only one personal fee is payable however many attempts are made to connect the call during any period of 24 hours.

Freefone This service encourages people to get in touch with a business. It is a very convenient and excellent service for business as it opens up a new way of stimulating orders, enquiries and information. Clients and agents can telephone the organization without cost to themselves. Freefone callers dial the operator and quote the firm's freefone number. Connection is without charge but the organization is charged the price of the call plus a small fee. The receptionist *must* accept the call.

Transfer charge call The receptionist may, on occasion, be asked to accept and pay for a call. She should refuse unless the caller is known to, or employed by, the organization as transfer charge calls are very expensive.

Credit card services The telephone credit card service enables individuals to make calls from any telephone, including a coinbox, without payment at the time. Credit cards will be charged to the firm's telephone account. Each card has a special number which must be quoted when the call is made.

Charges for Inland Calls
(including calls to the Channel Islands and Irish Republic)

Call Charge Letter	Type of Call	Charge Rate	Dialled direct						Connected by the Operator	
			Time allowed for unit charge of 4p excl VAT (4.6p incl VAT) on any one call	Approximate cost of call, including VAT, for:					For first 3 minutes or part (approx cost of call including VAT shown in brackets)	
				1 min	3 mins	5 mins	10 mins		Normal charge	Lower charge
L	Local Calls	Peak	2 mins	5p	9p	14p	23p		15p (17p)	6p* (7p*)
		Standard	3 mins	5p	5p	9p	18p		12p (14p)	4p* (5p*)
		Cheap	9 mins	**5p**	**5p**	**5p**	**9p**		**12p† (14p†)**	**4p† (5p†)**
a	Calls up to 56 km (35 miles) distance	Peak	30 secs	9p	28p	46p	92p		39p (45p)	24p (28p)
		Standard	45 secs	9p	18p	32p	64p		30p (35p)	15p (17p)
		Cheap	144 secs	**5p**	**9p**	**14p**	**23p**		**21p (24p)**	**4p* (5p*)**
b	Calls over 56 km (35 miles) distance	Peak	10 secs	28p	83p	£1.38	£2.76		87p (£1.00)	72p (83p)
		Standard	15 secs	18p	55p	92p	£1.84		63p (72p)	48p (55p)
		Cheap	48 secs	**9p**	**18p**	**32p**	**60p**		**30p (35p)**	**15p (17p)**
c	Calls to the Channel Islands	Peak	10 secs	28p	83p	£1.38	£2.76		87p (£1.00)	Normal charge applies
		Standard	10 secs	28p	83p	£1.38	£2.76		87p (£1.00)	Normal charge applies
		Cheap	24 secs	**14p**	**37p**	**60p**	**£1.15**		**45p (52p)**	Normal charge applies
	Calls to the Irish Republic (from Great Britain and Isle of Man)	Peak	8 secs	37p	£1.06	£1.75	£3.45		£1.05 (£1.21)	Normal charge applies
		Standard	8 secs	37p	£1.06	£1.75	£3.45		£1.05 (£1.21)	Normal charge applies
		Cheap	15 secs	**18p**	**55p**	**92p**	**£1.84**		**63p (72p)**	Normal charge applies

* each 3 minutes or part   † each 9 minutes or part

Peak Rate: Monday–Friday, 9 am–1 pm.
Standard Rate: Monday–Friday, 8 am–9 am and 1 pm–6 pm.
Cheap Rate: Weekends and all other times.

Notes

1 The charge for all calls connected by the operator is at the rate in force when the call is originated.

2 Unless otherwise shown, the charges for calls connected by the operator are for the first 3 minutes or part; each additional minute (or part) being ⅓ of the charge shown.

3 The **normal operator charge** applies to: special services (e.g. transferred charge calls, personal calls); calls which you choose not to dial yourself; calls subsequently connected by the operator after the caller in attempting to dial and the operator in attempting once to connect, have both received the engaged tone or no reply.

4 The **lower operator charge** applies to calls that have to be connected by the operator because the caller cannot dial or because a dialled call has failed.

5 Calls from Northern Ireland to the Irish Republic are at the appropriate inland rates.

6 All rates may be changed on certain days at Christmas and New Year.

Figure 23   Inland call charges (correct at time of printing)

Questions

1. What is
   a) STD
   b) IDD?
2. Give three ways of making a telephone call so that the recipient will pay for the call.
3. Give the names of four recorded services which may be obtained over the telephone and which would be of use to the business person.
4. What is
   a) an ADC call;
   b) a fixed time call;
   c) an alarm call?
5. In an emergency what number should the telephonist dial? Name the emergency services.
6. What is a personal call? Is it as useful a service now as it once was? If not, why not?

Assignment 10

1. Compare the prices of a fifteen minute telephone call from Oxford to Manchester on:
   Monday morning at 1100 hours;
   Tuesday afternoon at 1600 hours;
   Wednesday evening at 2100 hours.
   What does a caller save by delaying a morning call until the evening?
2. Look in the Green Pages of the telephone directory and find the name of the ten recorded services that are available to a subscriber. Find the telephone number of each recorded service (the centre nearest to you) and work out the cost for a one minute call to each one.
3. Now find the following telephone numbers:
   the local bus or coach station;
   the nearest main line train station;
   the local library;
   the citizen's advice bureau;
   the nearest information centre;
   the local police station.

17 Telephone equipment

To be really efficient the receptionist must have the correct equipment. To begin with the following aids are essential:
1 The local telephone directory;
2 The local classified telephone directory;
3 The STD booklet;
4 The IDD booklet;
5 An index of regularly used telephone numbers; a strip index is very useful here and this is described more fully in the chapter on filing and indexing;
6 The London directories (if the organization is based out of London) as so many important organizations have their offices in the capital.

There are three types of switchboard that a telephonist may be required to operate.

PBX stands for Private Branch Exchange. This is an internal telephone system only and is not connected with the Post Office telephone system. In the majority of organizations more than three quarters of the calls are internal and the great advantage of PBX is that it leaves the outside lines free for incoming or outgoing calls. Extensions are connected by pressing the appropriate switch or button on the switchboard which will sound a buzzer in the appropriate office.

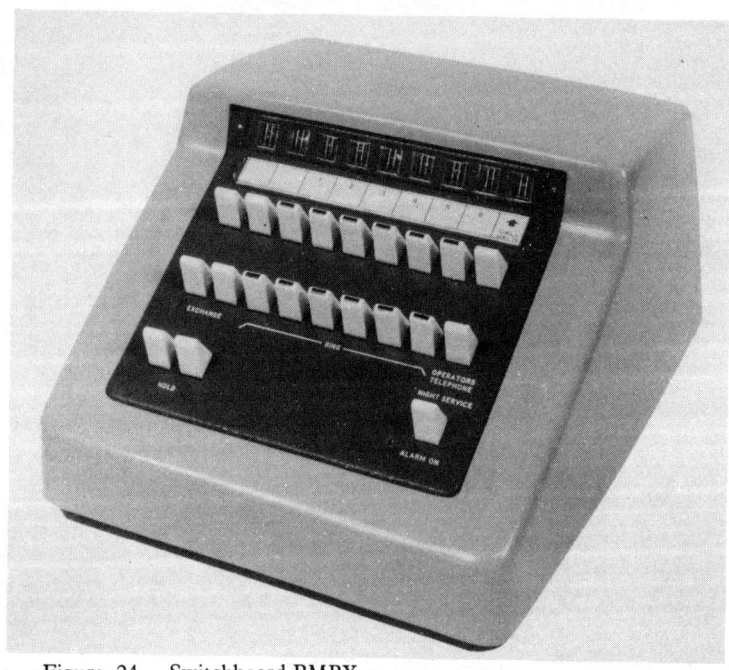

Figure 24 Switchboard PMBX

PMBX means Private Manual Branch Exchange. The smallest switchboard available deals with two exchange lines and six extensions. They can, of course, be very much larger and have up to six exchange lines and 24 extensions. The incoming calls are all routed by the operator. No extension telephone in any of the offices may make an outside call without asking the receptionist for a line. This has the advantage of monitoring outgoing calls and prevents personnel making expensive, private telephone calls.

PABX means Private Automatic Branch Exchange. These enable outgoing calls to be dialled direct from the extensions. The services available are as follows:

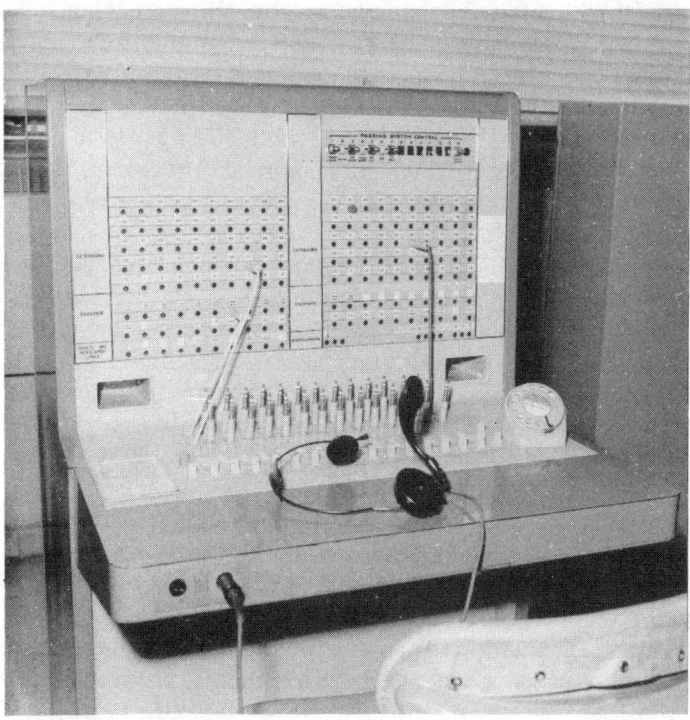

Figure 25   PMBX

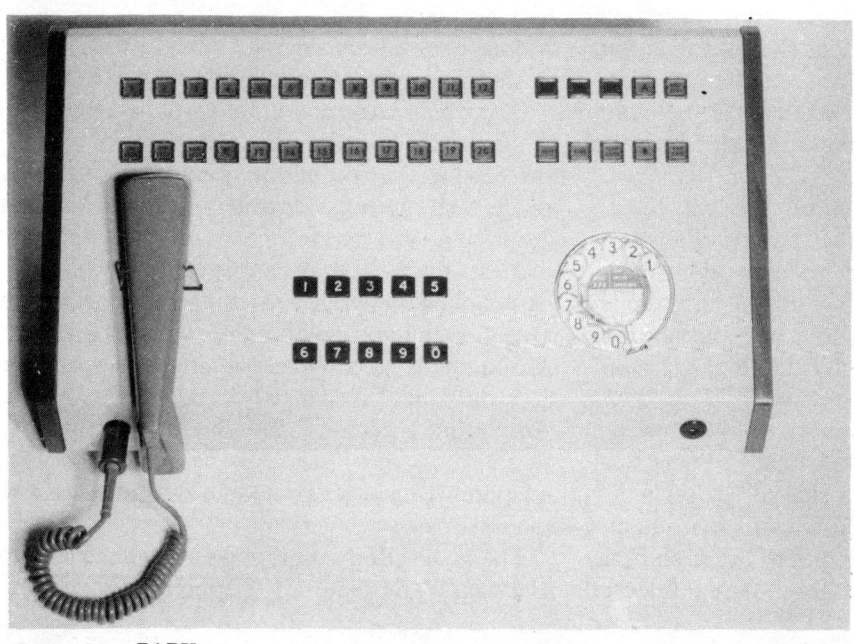

Figure 26   PABX

a) The consol (the PABX switchboard) combines internal and external telephones. Each member of staff may have external calls, calls from other offices within the building. The staff member can dial any colleague in any office and can, by dialling '9' be automatically connected with an outside line.

b) The receptionist may be reached by dialling '0'. She will often be asked to get a specified number for busy members of staff.

c) Meters to measure the length of calls may be installed at the switchboard. This is a very good deterrent to time and money wasting members of staff.

d) Sometimes an important incoming call may arrive when the extension is being used for an internal call. The receptionist may break into the internal call and offer the trunk call. As the receptionist breaks into the internal call a high pitched warning note operates to prevent the receptionist from overhearing what might well be confidential information.

e) There are 'waiting' circuits for callers who wish to wait until a member of staff has finished another outside call. When the member of staff replaces the receiver it will automatically pick up the waiting call.

f) It is possible to hold for enquiry. If a member of staff needs to confer with a colleague concerning a topic that has been raised by an outside caller the 'enquiry' button may be pressed. This enables the outside call to be held while an internal number can be dialled. When the member of staff has obtained an answer he or she may then 'cut' back to the original call.

g) Outside calls may be transferred automatically from one extension to another by pressing the 'enquiry' button.

The PABX switchboard is a veritable 'wizard' in the number of services that it offers. The procedures are made simple for the receptionist after her basic training. By viewing the illuminated panel she can see which lines are busy, which lines are waiting and which extentions are awaiting attention.

A loudspeaking telephone is a speakerset which amplifies incoming telephone calls. There is an amplifier on the left-hand side of the set which enables the user to have both hands free and also allows a number of personnel to listen and take part in, a telephone conversation. If a confidential call comes through, the handset at the back of the speakerset may be employed.

Intercommunication

The receptionist may find that she is employed in an organization where the personnel spend nearly all their time at their desks. In this case, the internal telephone system will be adequate for making internal contact. Another telephonist may find that her job is not quite so easy as the personnel in her organization have jobs which entail their moving around. Trying to locate them by internal telephone will be very tedious indeed so other methods of contacting personnel may be employed.

A small radio receiver which emits a shrill bleeping signal when activated may be carried in a pocket. The telephonist will activate the bleeper whenever she receives a telephone call or telephone message for the member of staff concerned and the 'bleep' will not cease until the contacted person goes to the nearest telephone to receive the message. This is called a paging device.

A public address system consists of a microphone, an amplifier and loudspeakers. The telephonist may call for a specific member of the staff by broadcasting through the organization via the microphone and amplifier at the telephonist's switchboard. All the telephonist needs to do is to ask the person concerned to go to the nearest telephone. She can then relay a message, or alternatively connect him or her with an outside caller. Messages of a more general nature to all members of staff may be transmitted by this method.

Occasionally telephone calls will be made to an organization after the end of the working day. In these cases the receptionist may employ a telephone answering machine. The telephone answering set is useful for receiving orders and requests for service. An answering set which can be switched on in place of the telephone will then give to individual callers a pre-recorded message. Messages may contain useful information and the recording may be changed as and when required. Answering machines may also be employed to receive messages. These may be dealt with by the telephonist or other personnel when they arrive the next day.

The card callmaker employs a punched card to dial calls. The required telephone numbers are 'punched' into plastic cards by special equipment. All the numbers on the plastic cards have a round scored hole which is very easy to push out. Once the numbers have been replaced by holes they may be stored in a special box. When wishing to use the card callmaker, the receptionist will select the correct card (easily identifiable as it has space for writing the name and the number of the person to be called) and drop it into the slot at the end of the callmaker. The callmaker is connected to the telephone and the card, when inserted, will work its way through the slot dialling the number automatically as it goes.

The tape callmaker is capable of storing up to 500 telephone numbers on magnetic tape. These two automatic callmakers are extremely useful to the busy receptionist-telephonist who needs to make a great many international calls. Mis-dialling on overseas calls can prove to be extremely costly and the two automatic dialling devices are absolutely foolproof.

A fairly new invention is ATLAS which stands for Automated Telephone Line Address System. This is extremely useful for the busy telephonist as it can be programmed with required calls for some hours ahead. The telephonist will look up the required codes and numbers and then feed them into the ATLAS storage bank by pressing the appropriate buttons. The pre-set numbers will be dialled automatically when the correct number is selected. When numbers are engaged the call will cancel after thirty seconds. This is not a permanent record and ATLAS is very useful because of this as the numbers may be changed to meet the current day's requirements.

New equipment

At the British Telecom research laboratories prototype communication devices are displayed which might almost be taken from the realms of science fiction!

There is a system of optical fibre voice transmission in which a strand of glass fibre no thicker than a human hair is capable of carrying 2000 telephone conversations simultaneously.

The latest invention is a fully electronic push-button telephone which is capable of storing in its memory bank all commonly-called numbers. It can be adjusted for loud or quiet ringing and, extremely useful, it can re-dial numbers that were engaged initially. This telephone, which is a mini-computer terminal, has rows of buttons, a visual display unit and even an electronic voice to give all the necessary instruction!

It will no longer be necessary for the receptionist to say 'Would you speak a little louder please, we appear to have a poor connection!' A plastic device in the telephone earpiece will eliminate static and make the contact at the other end of the line, whether he be in Brisbane or Nova Scotia, sound as if he is sitting in the same office.

The compuphone is a computer controlled telephone system. It has a memory bank which will remember up to one hundred, twelve digit numbers. These numbers may be dialled automatically after a three second interval.

There are three time zone clocks. One of these will always be on display. The other two can be read by the touch of a function key. All three are programmed and can be pre-set to either twelve hour or twenty-four hour time display. The telephone numbers, time and user input are displayed on a green fluorescent readout. The required number can be keyed in and visually checked. The dial button is then pressed in order to obtain the required number.

Questions

1. Name the six essential aids that a telephonist will need.
2. Name the three different types of switchboard.
3. What is
   a) pocket paging and
   b) a loud speaking telephone?
4. Describe an answering set and say why they are so useful to business people.
5. What is a card callmaker?
6. What is a public address system? For what kind of messages are these most useful?

18 Telephone technique

The telephone is so useful in business today that it would be difficult to think of managing without it. Executives are saved the time and the money that would be wasted on journeys by air and land that could prove unnecessary. They are also saved the sheer physical fatigue that constant travelling would produce. Nowadays it is possible to speak directly with individuals throughout the length and breadth of the United Kingdom and in most places abroad.

The telephone is personal, immediate and very often is the cheapest method of communication. It has the following advantages:

1 It is an extremely rapid method of communication.
2 It is personal, an individual link between business people.
3 It is relatively cheap.
4 Automatic answering devices may be employed to record and give messages when personnel have left the office.
5 It is an excellent method of communication when a two-way question and answer type of conversation is essential.

The telephonist must, in the same way as the receptionist, cultivate a pleasant, clear, well-modulated voice. With a telephonist however, it is even more important to cultivate a 'good' speaking voice. This means it must be clear, with no slurred consonants, flattened vowels or running of words and sentences together. The telephonist, like the receptionist, is the first link that the public has with her organization and she should deal with callers in a courteous, efficient manner. This gives the impression of a helpful, well-managed organization which will give good value for time and money spent. This is particularly true of hotel receptionists and telephonists. Potential customers are not likely to make reservations if their first contact with the hotel is with an apparently surly, ill-mannered telephonist.

When answering the telephone the telephonist should greet the caller with 'Good Morning' or 'Good Afternoon' and then give them the name of her organization. She should always greet callers brightly and make a point of addressing them by name once she knows what it is.

The telephonist should never employ slang words or familiarities, such as dear, but should use the following phrases:

1 Instead of 'O.K.' – she should say 'Certainly Mr/Mrs/Miss . . .'.
2 As an alternative to 'Hang on' the words 'Will you hold the line please . . .' or 'One moment please' will be far more acceptable to the caller.
3 The telephonist should never make bald statements to the caller such as – 'He's out'. 'I am sorry but Mr . . . is not in the office at the moment, can I take a message for you?' is far more helpful and leaves the caller feeling much more pleasantly disposed towards the organization.
4 Abrupt questions such as 'Mr. Who', 'What's that you said?' sound rude although the telephonist may not wish to give that impression. It is far better if she says 'Could you repeat that please?' – or – 'would you say that again, I'm sorry but I'm afraid that this line is not too clear.'

It is absolutely essential that a pen and a message pad is kept by the side of the telephone. Very often an executive is not in the office when required and the caller may like to leave a message. Messages must be accurately recorded and not left to memory.

The message pad should contain the following information:

1 The name of the person for whom the message is intended;
2 The name of the person leaving the message and the company;
3 His/her telephone number (for future reference – or – if he/she is required to be rung back);
4 The nature of the message (urgency and how delivered);
5 Whether the caller will ring or call back;
6 A summary of the message giving special attention to figures;
7 Date the message was received;
8 Time the message was received;
9 Signature of the individual who took the message.

Telephone Message

Date .... Time received ....

Telephone call for ....

Caller's name ....

Address ....

....

Telephone Number ....

Message ....

....

....

....

....

Received by ....

Figure 27   A telephone message pad

If the telephonist is disconnected she should replace the receiver as the individual making the call should ring through and establish a new connection as soon as he or she is able to do so. If the telephonist receives calls which are wrong numbers then she should accept the caller's apologies politely, remembering that it is equally as frustrating to the caller and that wrong numbers are never called intentionally.

If it is necessary to leave the telephone to collect information for a caller, ensure that he or she is told what is causing the delay in answering his or her query, and how long the delay is likely to be. Sometimes a caller will prefer to ring back rather than wait for answers to questions or for bookings to be verified. It would be a nice gesture on the part of the telephonist to ring the caller once she has obtained the necessary information. When an incoming call has to be transferred from one part of the building to another, the caller's message or request should be conveyed to the new extension so that he or she does not have to give the same message all over again. Callers find this particularly irksome, especially if they are passed from department to department.

When making telephone calls the telephonist should ensure that she has the correct code and number before dialling. When making international calls the telephonist should follow these basic rules.

1 Before commencing to dial the complete number should be noted. The telephonist should never rely on her memory when making international calls as it is too expensive to risk getting the wrong number.
2 When dialling, the telephonist should ensure that there are no long pauses between figures – if there are, the call may fail.
3 The telephonist should allow some time for her call to get through remembering that it is passing through many sets of equipment over very long distances.

Tones in other countries that tell whether a number is ringing or engaged are often different from those in this country. For a free demonstration of commonly heard tones the telephonist may dial 100 and ask for Freefone 2070 for those tones used in Europe and Freefone 2071 for those used in North America.

The telephonist will, no doubt, be familiar with the tones in Britain. They are:

1 Dialling tone is a low pitched, smooth 'burr'.
2 A repeated double 'purr' tells that the number is being rung.
3 A single high-pitched note repeated at regular intervals will tell the telephonist that the number that she is ringing is engaged.
4 A continuous high-pitched note means that the number is unobtainable. If the telephonist is sure that she is dialling the right number then she should ring '100' and let the telephone operator know of the difficulty.
5 A series of high-pitched rapid notes means that the call is coming from a 'pay phone'. The telephonist should allow the caller time to insert money in the box.

When dialling, the telephonist should ensure that she dials correctly by taking the dial right round to the fingerstop and allowing it to run back freely each time she dials a figure. If a mistake is made while dialling, the telephonist should replace the receiver briefly before re-dialling. If the telephonist is connected to the wrong number she should apologise. If she finds that she has constant trouble with one particular number she may dial 100 and ask the operator to obtain the number for her. The telephonist should be aware, however, that operator connected calls are more expensive than the calls made on STD.

A telephone call should be planned so that all relevant points are discussed and no time is wasted. When words are in doubt the telephone alphabet should be employed. Words should be spelled using the appropriate word of the telephone alphabet for each letter.

The telephone alphabet

A	Alpha	N	November
B	Bravo	O	Oscar
C	Charlie	P	Papa
D	Delta	Q	Quebec
E	Echo	R	Romeo
F	Foxtrot	S	Sierra
G	Golf	T	Tango
H	Hotel	U	Uniform
I	India	V	Victor
J	Juliette	W	Whisky
K	Kilo	X	X-ray
L	Lima	Y	Yanky
M	Mike	Z	Zulu

When working at the switchboard the telephonist will, at times, be very busy indeed and it is essential that she keeps calm and does not 'panic'. A flustered telephonist is going to mis-dial, cut off outgoing calls, incoming calls and calls between the extensions. She will also be inclined to connect personnel to the wrong extensions. This will only increase her confusion. A pleasant 'I'm sorry to keep you waiting', or 'Hold the line one moment please' is all that is needed provided, of course, that the delay is not too long and that she keeps in contact with waiting callers to let them know that she hasn't forgotten them.

The telephonist must 'monitor' all calls so that the executives within her organization are not constantly bothered with trivial queries and routine questions. A telephonist's technique may be something like this:

Telephonist: 'Good morning, Jones Brothers Ltd. Can I help you?'
Caller: 'Good morning, may I speak to Mr Braithwaite please?'
Telephonist: 'Could I have your name please sir?'
Caller: 'Yes, this is John Drew of Windowlite.'
Telephonist: 'One moment Mr Drew, I'll see if Mr Braithwaite is in his office.'

Now the telephonist will place Mr Drew's call on the 'Waiting circuit' so that he cannot hear her conversation with Mr Braithwaite. She will then ring Mr Braithwaite's extension.

Telephonist: 'I have Mr Drew of "Windowlite" on the line for you Mr Braithwaite.'
Mr Braithwaite: 'I can't talk to him now, I'm far too busy at the moment. Get him to ring back would you?'

The telephonist will then disconnect the call to Mr Braithwaite's office and will cut into the waiting circuit where Mr Drew is holding.

Telephonist: 'I am sorry Mr Drew but I'm afraid that Mr Braithwaite is not in his office at the moment. He should be in later if you would care to ring back then — or — I can take a message if you wish.'

Whatever Mr Drew decides to do about leaving a message he will do so amicably. His feeling are

not hurt as he had no way of knowing exactly what Mr Braithwaite did say. Mr Braithwaite has not been bothered by telephone calls that he has not time to cope with. A telephonist's task then is two-fold:
1 to shield her senior staff and
2 to deal tactfully with all callers.

When making outgoing calls for members of staff the telephonist's task might be something like this:
On seeing an extension signal flash she will plug into it

Telephonist: 'Yes, Mr Treward, can I help you?'
Mr Treward: 'Get me "Euphonics of Dagenham" will you?'

Here the telephonist will have to look up the number of 'Euphonics'. If it is an often-dialled number, then she will, no doubt, have her own record of it on a strip index or a card index. If she has not got the number listed in her own personal files then she will have to look it up. If her local exchange is Dagenham then she will look up 'Euphonics' under the alphabetical list of subscribers in her local telephone directory. If, however, Dagenham is *not* her local exchange then she will need some help in finding their number.

Baker, HG 23 Broad Street, Oxford	0623 563802
Barnes, KP Shirley High Street, Southampton	0703 567923
Bell, William Kimberly Rd. Falmouth	315674
Brewer, JA High St. Falmouth	315914
Brown Bros. Kernick St. Penryn	36 78649
Butler Verner Ltd. Fareham, Hants	0806 54654

Figure 28 A strip index

All telephone numbers may be obtained from Directory Enquiries – 102 for numbers in London and 192 for those outside London. When directory enquiries answers, on 192, the telephonist must give the name of the exchange that is required, Dagenham, followed by the name and the address of the subscriber. When she is given the number by directory enquiries she should write it down and then repeat it to ensure that she has heard correctly. She will then look up the appropriate code for Dagenham in her STD codebook and dial it, followed by the number given to her by directory enquiries.

When Euphonics answer, the telephonist will ring Mr Treward's office and inform him that she has his call, connect him and take herself off the line so that she does not hear the ensuing conversation. When the call is finished, Mr Treward's extension light will flash and the telephonist will then disconnect the call.

When answering machines are employed to receive messages in an office it may well be the task of the telephonist to deal with these recorded messages and requests when she arrives at work in the morning.

She will re-play the tapes and obtain the information left on the answering machine since the close of business on the previous evening. A message pad must be employed for each separate message and the tape should be replayed to verify that the information has been taken down correctly. Each message must be delivered to the person named or, if not named, then to the member of staff who is most likely to be concerned. Again, the telephonist needs a thorough knowledge of the firm's organizational structure and each member of staff's responsibilities.

Questions

1. What are the advantages of using the telephone as a method of communication?
2. Suggest alternatives for the following
    a) Hang on . . .
    b) O.K.
    c) Hullo.
    d) He's out.
    e) Say that again!
3. What information should a message pad contain?
4. What are the basic rules to follow when dialling international calls?
5. What is the telephone alphabet and when would it be employed?
6. Why must a receptionist monitor all calls?
7. How can a telephonist discover a subscriber's number when he or she is not listed in the local telephone directory?
8. Why must a caller be placed upon a waiting circuit while waiting to be connected to an extension?

Assignment 11

You are the switchboard operator in your firm and have to take many messages for members of staff who are out on business. Take each of the following messages, record it on a message sheet, using your initiative concerning dates and times. Make use of the organization chart to find any extension numbers.
Messages for:

1. Mr T Bright – The log books for the vehicles, TWD 619 W and HAA 202 W are now due from Abbey Garages of Long Handborough, Oxford.
2. Mr L Shaw – From Selbourne Office Supplies. No thermal stencils were included on this month's order. Is this an oversight?
3. Mr I Sutherland – There are no spares available for the grinder LK/6/71. Would Mr Sutherland please contact W L Angove and let him know whether he wishes the firm to get supplies from other sources. W L Angove's number is 0703 783821.
4. Mr L Jenkins – Would Mr Jenkins please phone Miss Barbara Stimpson of *The Southern Daily Echo* as there is a query on Friday's advertising copy.
5. Mr N Rosser – Mr Jeffreys of Scarr & Winthrop, Accountants wishes to cancel his appointment on Friday, 12th. Would Mr Rosser please ring Mr Jeffrey at 0703 619391 to arrange another appointment.
6. Telephone message from Mrs Lilian Clarke asking for her P60.
   Message to Wages Department, Mrs M Lovegrove.
7. Two rush orders for Peabody and Grace of Dorking.
   3 dozen boxes of carbons
   50 reams of Bond A4 typing paper
   25 reams of Bond A5 typing paper
   35 reams of A4 bank paper
   16 reams of A5 bank typing paper
   10 reams of duplicating paper
   If this order cannot be delivered by the 11th would the ordering department please ring Peabody and Grace 0803 56 7456.
8. Mr H Browning – Please telephone Hugh Margetts (Oxford 74343 Ext 176). Mr Simpson would like to speak to him also about the appointment he made to call and see him on Tuesday of next week. Mr Simpson's number is Didcot 78965.

19 Routing calls

The telephonist should know precisely how to route calls. Very seldom will she answer the telephone switchboard and find that the caller knows precisely to whom he or she wishes to speak. More often than not the telephone conversation will sound something like this:

Telephonist: 'Good morning, Jones Brothers Limited, can I help you?'

Caller: 'Hullo – I want to know why the spare parts for my photocopier haven't arrived. They were promised last week and the darned machine is lying idle. Can you let me know if they are on the way. It is getting very urgent and it really isn't good enough. I thought that you people were supposed to be reliable.'

Telephonist: 'Would you give me your name please sir?'

Caller: 'John Smith of Tebrason.'

Telephonist: 'Would you hold the line please Mr Smith and I will connect you to our Sales Manager, Mr Duffy.'

The telephonist will then ring extension 17 (see chart, page 76) and inform Mr Duffy in the following manner:

Telephonist: 'Mr Duffy, I have Mr John Smith of Tebrason on the line. He was promised some spare parts for his photocopier a week ago. They haven't arrived yet and he is a little irate.'

Mr Duffy: 'Thank-you, will you put him through.'

Telephonist: 'You are through to Mr Duffy, Mr Smith.'

Notice the way that the telephonist:
1 Gave the caller his name as soon as she knew what it was;
2 Knew exactly to whom she should connect the caller;
3 Stated the caller's request to Mr Duffy so that
a) the caller did not need to repeat himself,
b) Mr Duffy knew precisely what the problem was.

Again the telephone rings and the telephonist will answer in the usual way.

Caller: 'I've got a mistake on my last statement. You say that I owe you £240 from last month and I've already paid that amount. Could you . . .

Telephonist: (interrupting politely) If I could have your name sir, I'll put you through to our Accounts Department.

Having ascertained the caller's name she will then ring the Sales Accounts department on extension 12. (see chart)

Telephonist: 'Mr Abrahmas, I have Mr Stimpson on the line. He has an overcharge on his last statement.'

Again, the receptionist has passed along the relevant information to the correct department. The matter can then be speedily and amicably resolved. The telephonist, in both cases, has smoothed over the situation by her efficiency and tact.

Supposing that the telephonist had only a very incomplete knowledge of her firm's organizational structure, this is what *could* (and often does) happen.

Let us take Mr Smith's call again.

Telephonist: 'Hullo.'

Caller: 'Is that Jones Brothers?'

Telephonist: 'Yes.'

Caller: 'I want to know why the spare parts for my photo-copier etc.

Telephonist: 'Hang on.'
She will then wonder where spare parts are dealt with – decide that it is probably the stores and will connect Mr Smith with the stores (ext 30)

Stores: 'Stores – Ryle speaking.'
Telephonist: 'Call for you,' and to Mr Smith, 'You're through.'
Mr Ryle: 'Hullo – can I help you?'
Caller: 'Hullo, I am calling about my spare parts.'
Mr Ryle: 'What spare parts sir?'
Caller: 'Those for my photo-copier! I've just been explaining to somebody else that my photo-copier is out of action. You promised faithfully that I should have those parts by the end of last week and what has happened – nothing. Let me . . .
Mr Ryle: (Interrupting) 'Sorry sir but I think that you are through to the wrong department. Hold the line and I'll put you back to the switchboard.'

He recalls the switchboard and asks to have the call transferred to the Sales department. The telephonist transfers the call.

Mr Duffy: 'Hullo, Sales Department.'
Caller: 'Now look here – are you or are you not going to get those spare parts out to me today?'
Mr Duffy: 'Could I have your name sir?'
Caller: 'Smith' – he is, by now, so angry that he is practically shouting. 'Look here, I'm trying to find somebody who knows something about my order. Nobody seems to know anything, or even care. It really is too bad and it's the very last time that your firm will get any business from me!'

Mr Duffy may, by attempting to placate Mr Smith with profuse apologies and with a promise of immediate delivery of the missing spare parts, manage to soothe him. None of this would have been necessary, however, if the telephonist had known of the responsibilities of each member of staff. She should also know who is in a position to deputize should a member of staff be absent.

For instance, if Mr Duffy had been out of his office when Mr Smith's query had come through, the telephonist would know that the Chief Sales Representative, (Mr. Hannon) would be able to deal with the problem as he acts as Mr Duffy's deputy when Mr Duffy is not available.

The telephonist should keep a copy of the organization chart over her switchboard. This should show:

1 The structure of the organization;
2 The heads of the departments, their telephone extension numbers and their room allocation;
3 The responsibility of each member of staff;
4 An alphabetical cross reference for ease of location.

When outside callers announce that they wish to speak to the Managing Director, the General Manager or the Company Secretary then the receptionist should contact that executive's personal secretary. She will deal with all her employer's routine calls. The personal secretary will screen all calls and pass only those that she knows should be dealt with personally.

Assignment 12

You are a receptionist-telephonist for a medium sized manufacturing company. It would be of great help to you in locating specific members of staff if you could have a chart showing:

1 Departmental Managers and their Departments;
2 Responsibility of each Manager.

Draw up an organization chart. Show how the departments are responsible for certain areas by saying where you would place the following calls.

1 A query on an invoice
2 An order
3 Non-payment of a bill
4 Application for employment
5 Query regarding a sales advertisement
6 Query regarding spare parts for machinery
7 Query regarding despatch of goods
8 Appointment required to discuss insurance claim
9 Query regarding employee's sick pay
10 Query from the auditors

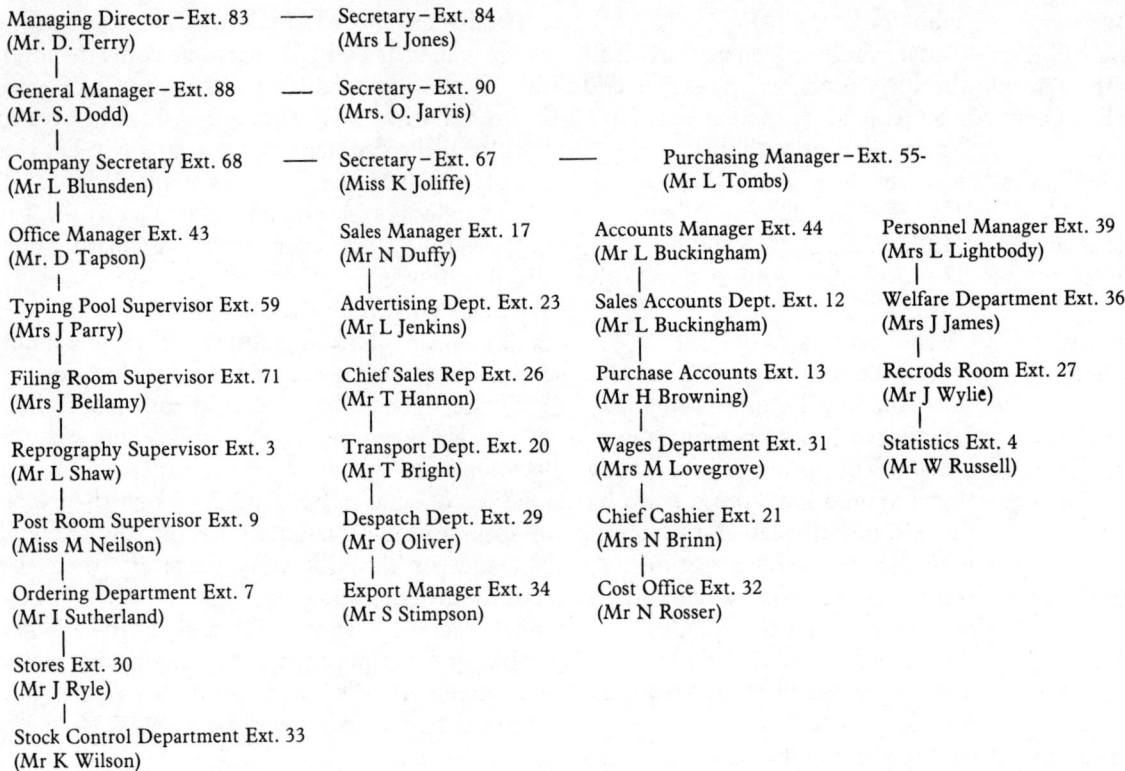

Figure 29   An organization chart

1	Abraham, S.	Ext. 12	Sales Accounts
2	Bellamy, Mrs J.	Ext. 68	Filing room supervisor
3	Blunsden, L.	Ext. 71	Company Secretary
4	Bright, T.	Ext. 20	Transport department
5	Brinn, Mrs N.	Ext. 21	Chief Cashier
6	Browning, H.	Ext. 13	Purchase Accounts
7	Buckingham, L.	Ext. 44	Accounts Manager
8	Dodd, S.	Ext. 88	General Manager
9	Duffy, N.	Ext. 17	Sales Manager
10	Hannon, T.	Ext. 26	Chief Sales Representative
11	Hill, Mrs P.	Ext. 57	Secretary to Purchasing Manager
12	James, Mrs J.	Ext. 36	Welfare
13	James, Mrs O	Ext. 90	Secretary to General Manager
14	Jenkins, L.	Ext. 23	Advertising Department
15	Joliffe, Mrs J.	Ext. 67	Secretary to Mr. Blunsden
16	Jones, Mrs L.	Ext. 84	Secretary to Managing Director
17	Lightbody, J.	Ext. 39	Personnel Manager
18	Lovegrove, Mrs M.	Ext. 31	Wages department
19	Neilson, Mrs M.	Ext. 9	Post room supervisor
20	Oliver, A.	Ext. 29	Despatch department
21	Parry, Mrs J.	Ext. 59	Typing room supervisor
22	Rosser, Miss N.	Ext. 32	Cost office
23	Russell, W.	Ext. 4	Statistics
24	Ryle, J.	Ext. 30	Stores
25	Shaw, L.	Ext. 3	Reprography supervisor
26	Stimpson, S.	Ext. 34	Export manager
27	Sutherland, I.	Ext. 7	Ordering department
28	Tapson, D.	Ext. 43	Office Manager
29	Terry, D.	Ext. 83	Managing Director
30	Tombs, L.	Ext. 55	Purchasing Manager
31	Wilson, K.	Ext. 33	Stock control department
32	Wylie, J	Ext. 27	Records department

Figure 30   An alphabetic cross-reference list

20 Other methods of communication

Receptionists need to be able to communicate with personnel in various ways. The telephone is, of course, the most widely used method of communication in an organization but in addition to the efficient, capable handling of the switchboard and intercom systems, the receptionist should know how and when it would be appropriate to use other methods.

Memoranda

It is occasionally important for staff to be informed of an important fact or given instructions in writing. In these circumstances a memorandum form is employed. Notice that the memorandum has no salutation or complimentary close. The main points are:

MEMORANDUM

TO: All REPRESENTATIVES
FROM: MR A BENSON
DATE: 20th March 19..

SUBJECT Representatives' Expense Accounts

Would all Sales Representatives please ensure that their monthly expenses are presented to this department on the last day of each month.

Would representatives also please note that their new telephone credit cards are now available for collection.

AB

Figure 31   A memorandum

1 Who is it from?
2 To whom is it addressed?
3 Date;
4 Brief subject matter.

No confidential information would ever be relayed by this method.

The telex system

Some receptionists are required to operate a teleprinter which can send and receive typewritten information.

The teleprinter has a keyboard like that on a typewriter and a dialling unit like that of a telephone; it is therefore known as the typewriting telephone. It combines the speed of the telephone and the reliability of the written word. Because it is so fast and so reliable it is widely used, not only in Britain, but throughout the world.

Indeed it has very great value when employed internationally. Direct communication between this country and some countries abroad is very difficult because office personnel are working different hours. Provided that the teleprinter is left switched on, it may receive messages from all over the world throughout the night. These messages may be attended to immediately the receptionist arrives at the office the next morning.

The speed of the transmission (the speed of actually sending the call) will be that of the operator's typing so it is obviously important that a teleprinter operator is a trained typist, one who is accurate and has a good typing speed.

Teleprinters may be fitted with punched tape attachments which greatly speed up the transmission time. The punch tape attachment is incorporated into the left hand side of the teleprinter and this will produce messages in a special code on to punch tape. This special perforating attachment will combine the function of perforating the tape with typing a printed copy of the message. When the teleprinter operator has finished perforating the tape she can then fix it to the transmitter and send the message it contains at 70 wpm. It is, of course, only the message that is transmitted and not the punch tape.

Some organizations do not require the full facilities of telex so they may have a private teleprinter installation. These private installations are installed in the Head Office and Branch Offices of a Company. They are directly linked with a private line. These private lines teleprinters are hired from the Post Office in exactly the same way as the telex and the telephones.

The Post Office will provide a telex directory which gives the name of the telex subscriber and the number. It is used in exactly the same way as the telephone directory.

The advantages of the telex system far outweigh the disadvantages.

Advantages
1 The speed of the telephone
2 The reliability of the letter
3 Less time-wasting than the telephone because it eliminates the social chatter.
4 Easy to communicate directly with countries abroad in spite of the time differences.
5 Carbon copies of the message may be automatically made.

Disadvantages
1 Valuable transmission time may be wasted by inefficient operators.
2 Rapid two-way question and answer communication is difficult.
3 It is not suitable for confidential information as the telerinter messages are taken by the operator.
4 Difficult to judge authenticity of message as it is not signed.

Procedure for operating the teleprinter
1 Switch on.

Figure 32 A teleprinter

2 Dial the required number located in the telex directory, if necessary.
3 Receive the answer-back code. By this answer-back code she will know that she is through to the correct organization.
4 Send her own answer-back code. By this the other teleprinter operator will know who is in contact.
5 Send the message.
6 Send own answer-back code. This tells the other operator that the message is finished.
7 Receive the answer-back code from the receiving teleprinter. This will show that the line was open until the end of the message and that it was transmitted fully.
8 Clear the line so that the teleprinter may receive any incoming calls.

All telex messages might look something like this.

DOBBS FLW
DOBBS LDN
BOAT SS ARIADNE NOW DUE SOUTHAMPTON AT 1600 HOURS. CONSIGNMENT 4/619 SHOULD BE CLEARED CUSTOMS BY 2000 HOURS. PLEASE ARRANGE FOR IMMEDIATE COLLECTION.
1200
24 4 19--.
COL 1600 4/619 2000 1200 24 4 19--.
DOBBS LDN
DOBBS FLW

Telegrams

The Post Office's Telegraph Service provides a very rapid method of sending printed messages and these are known as telegrams. The usual method of sending a telegram is to write it on a special telegram form and hand it over the post office counter. A stock of forms may be kept in reception for this purpose.

A very concise message should be prepared and all words that are not strictly necessary should be eliminated. The message, however, should not be so abbreviated that the receiver of the telegram has difficulty in knowing what it means. The cost of the telegram is calculated on the number of words used plus the basic charge.

A telegraphic address should be used when this is known as it cuts down the number of words in the telegram. A telegraphic address is especially shortened for this purpose and must be registered with the post office.

The form should be filled in in capital letters and if it is typed then three spaces should be left between each word. A carbon copy should be taken for the files and a letter confirming the telegram should be despatched without delay. The sender's name and address should always be written on the back of the form.

The receptionist might be asked to send the following message by telegram:

Could you please contact Martins of Lancaster and tell them that we must have those spare parts for the Offset as soon as possible. Our brochures are held up and work in general is behind schedule. Ask them to let us know as soon as they have shipped the parts to us.
H. Baines.

MARTINS SUPPRINTS LANCASTER
SPARE PARTS FOR OFFSET
REQUIRED SOONEST STOP
WORK BEHIND SCHEDULE STOP
ADVISE
BAINES

The receptionist must cost out the telegram remembering the following points:
1 A word of more than 15 letters is counted as two words;
2 Figures are counted as 5 figures to a word;
3 Acceptable abbreviations such as UK count as one word;
4 Punctuation counts as one word.

A receptionist may telephone a telegram by dialling the correct number. The number to be dialled will be found in the front of the telephone directory. She must let the operator know her own telephone number and then she must dictate the message very clearly using the telephone alphabet if necessary. The post office operator will read the message back and the receptionist must check that reading with her own copy from which she dictated the telegram. The date and the exact time should be noted on the copy before it is filed away for reference.

A telegram may also be sent by telex. The correct number to use to send telegrams is supplied to the telex subscriber in the dialling code cards.

A telexed telegram when sent to a telex address will be delivered at any time, day or night, providing that the teleprinter is left switched on.

Other telegraph services

1 *Priority telegrams* may take precedence over others for a small extra charge.
2 *Confidential telegrams* must be marked as such and the word Confidential will appear on the envelope when delivered.
3 *Overnight telegrams* may be sent up to midnight and are delivered by first post the next morning. This is a cheaper service.
4 *Pre-paid telegrams* may be sent whereby the sender pays for a reply. A reply voucher is delivered with the telegram.
5 *Multiple telegrams* may be sent at a reduced charge to a number of addressees. The message must be identical and they must be delivered in the same postal area.
6 *Overseas telegrams* may be sent to most parts of the world, to ships in port, aircraft at airports and trains at railway stations.

There is therefore a method of communication for every situation and it is up to the receptionist to employ the method most suitable at the time and under the circumstances.

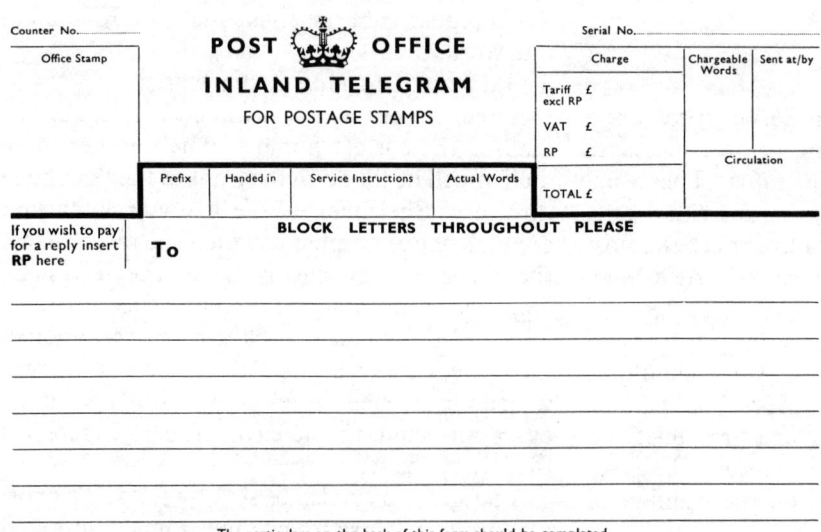

Figure 34 An inland telegram form

Questions

1. What are the main points of a memorandum?
2. The teleprinter is sometimes called the typewriting telephone. Explain this statement.
3. What are the advantages of employing a teleprinter to send messages?
4. What, if any, are the disadvantages of this method of communication?
5. Why is punched tape often used when transmitting a teleprinter message?
6. What is
   a) a priority telegram
   b) an overnight telegram
   c) a prepaid telegram
   d) an overseas telegram?

Assignment 13

Your sales manager becomes irate when important orders are lost because of the relative slowness of the post. He becomes positively angry when telephone orders are not recorded correctly, or even worse, when they are not passed on to the appropriate personnel.

1. Suggest two ways of overcoming these difficulties.
2. Draw a procedure chart for sending information by
   a) telephone
   b) teleprinter.
3. Compare telephones, teleprinters and telegrams under the following headings:
   a) cost;
   b) suitability for rapid two-way communication;
   c) reliability of information;
   d) sending figures and other complicated information.
4. State the main advantage of each of the three methods of communication.
5. State the main disadvantage for each method.

Part 5
Business procedures

21 The post

When the post arrives at the reception desk it must be carefully sorted into three distinct piles:
1. private and confidential mail;
2. first class mail;
3. second class mail.

In addition the receptionist should sign for all registered and recorded delivery letters and list them in a special ledger which is kept for this purpose.

Private and confidential mail should not be opened but should be delivered intact to the addressee. First class mail should be opened with a flat knife and slit neatly along the upper edge of the envelope. The receptionist should 'tap' the contents to the bottom of the envelope to avoid damaging the letter or any of the enclosures. The letters should be opened out flat and all enclosures should be checked and pinned to the letter which should then be date-stamped. This safeguards the firm against complaints if the mail is delayed in the post.

Very often the enclosures are remittances and these should be treated very carefully. The receptionist should ensure that the amount of money quoted in the body of the letter really has been enclosed. She should then list all the remittances

Date	Remitter	Ref.	Amount (£)	Method
3rd May	Johnson	619	31.46	Cheque
	Carpenter	k31	0.05	Stamps
	Day	450	1.60	Postal Order
	Stewart	k51	14.30	Cheque
	Lemon	k57	3.60	Cash (Reg)
	Keen	k13	48.00	Credit Transfer
	Rippington	k23	13.11	Cheque
	Notley	k21	16.60	Cheque
	Senior	k80	44.12	Girocheque
	North	566	0.56	Postal Order
	Knight	638	14.63	Cheque
	Law	714	11.90	Cash (Reg)

Signature ....
Checked by ....
Date ....

Figure 35   A page from a remittances book

received in the special book kept for this, the remittances book. If correct then the remittance book and all the remittances should be sent to the cashier.

The mail should then be sorted into departments. Pigeon holes are often used for sorting with separate pigeon holes for each department or departmental manager. (When hotel receptionists are dealing with the mail for their guests, they must, of course, place the letters in the appropriate pigeon holes without opening them.)

Second class mail is dealt with in the same way as first class mail and all empty envelopes should be checked to ensure that there is nothing remaining inside before they are discarded.

The receptionist will sometimes find that magazines, journals and periodicals arrive in the morning mail and need to be seen by several members of staff. A routine slip is affixed to each one and delivered to the first person on the list. When he or she has finished with the item the routing slip will be initialled and passed on, together with the magazine, to the next person on the list.

Occasionally a letter needs to be seen by more than one department. If the matter is urgent then the receptionist may take a photocopy of the letter so that each person concerned may have a copy simultaneously. If there is no urgency, however, a routing slip may be employed in the manner described above.

The receptionist will not wish to stay late every evening dealing with the post in a last minute rush to get it off on time. She must organize a definite procedure so that the mail is dealt with each day by a set time. This must be the deadline and the staff should be aware that mail which is not ready for the receptionist by the deadline

STAMPS BOUGHT	DATE 1981	ADDRESS AND TOWN	AMOUNT	REMARKS
£2.80	b/f			
£10.00	3/5			
£12.80		Freestones, Abingdon	0.85	Parcel
		Bray/Whitehead, Oxford	0.12	
		Brinn, Hamble	0.12	
		Partington, Botley	0.12	
		Keales, Southampton	0.12	
		Sales Reps.	3.00	30 x 10
		Mays, Edinburgh	0.12	
		Jenkins, Liverpool	0.12	Registered
		Veal, Portsmouth	0.12	
		Fanshaw, Bournemouth	1.58	Recorded
		Farr, Basingstoke	0.85	
		Madsen, London E4	0.10	
		Jones, Cardiff	0.69	Parcel
		Van Dieren, New York	0.22	Airmail
		Total	£8.13	
		Bal c/f	£4.67	
£12.80			£12.80	

Figure 36   Post book entries

must be left until the next day. Occasionally, of course, she will have to make exceptions, but these should be *exceptions* and not the general rule.

The receptionist, or a messenger, should collect the mail at fairly regular intervals so that it may be dealt with if there are slack moments in reception.

Some firms place the letters and enclosures in the envelopes and seal them before sending them down to the reception desk. Other firms will pin the letters and the enclosures to the envelope. In the latter case, the inside address and the address on the envelope should agree and the remittances should be checked to ensure that the right number are attached. If there are any discrepancies in either case, then the letter, envelope and the enclosures must be returned to the typist. On no account should the receptionist alter anything herself.

Outgoing mail should be sorted into:
1 First class mail;
2 Second class mail;
3 Overseas mail;
4 Special mail such as recorded and registered letters.

Some letters which are bulky will need to be weighed so that the correct postage may be affixed. An up-to-date Post Office Guide may be obtained from The Post Office. This is a valuable reference book (see Chapter 4) and is essential for the receptionist so that she can check on current postal charges. Stamps of the correct value must be affixed to each letter as the addressee will have to pay a surcharge on the mail delivered if the receptionist understamps it. Details of all mail, together with the value of the stamps used, must be recorded in the post book.

The postage account is balanced each day. The stamps should be locked away when not in use, otherwise it is tempting for other members of staff who 'borrow' stamps for their own private mail.

Some organizations may prefer to use a franking machine for prepaying the mail instead of using stamps. A franking machine will automatically print a gummed label with the correct value as well as the cancellation.

Franking machines may be hired or bought and a licence must be obtained for their use from the post office. The franking machine will record the value of the stamp on the meter. Credit units may be purchased by taking the meter from the franking machine along to the post office and paying the required amount. The meter is set to the required amount of credit units and locked into the franking machine by the post office clerk. The credit units are then deducted from the total amount each time a letter is franked. The receptionist may see at a glance precisely how much credit is remaining in the franking machine.

A docket must be filled out each day showing the amount of total units used, total units purchased and amount of units left in credit. The docket must be taken to the post office each week for checking. This prevents fraud.

The receptionist must ensure that the lever on the franking machine is set at the correct amount of postage, otherwise a great deal of money may be wasted if the first class mail is franked for, say, 140 pence instead of 14 pence.

A franking machine is quicker to use than loose stamps and is a very good accounting method. The problem is, however, that there is no record of outgoing mail as there is with a post book. If such a list were required then it would have to be made up separately.

Questions

1. Into what categories should the morning mail initially be sorted?
2. What is a remittance book?
3. Describe a routing slip and say what it is used for.
4. Why does a receptionist need to instigate a definite procedure for the collection of outgoing mail?
5. Why does some outgoing mail need to be weighed?
6. What is the main advantage of keeping a post book?
7. What is the main advantage of a franking machine? Are there any disadvantages?
8. What reference book is considered essential when dealing with the post?

Assignment 14

You have received in this morning's post the following mail:

26 first class letters comprising:
URGENT to the General Manager
PRIVATE & CONFIDENTIAL Sales Manager
2 PERSONAL letters (Sales and Production Managers.)
1 FOR THE ATTENTION OF PERSONNEL DEPT
Twelve orders
Two complaints
Four letters of application
Quotation worked IMMEDIATE
Letter from firm's auditors
Letter from firm's solicitors

12 second class letters:

7 invoices
2 statements of account
1 circular re stationery
1 electricity bill
1 letter from Inland Revenue
Two Registered letters for the Company Secretary, marked PRIVATE
Three Recorded Delivery letters:
2 for the accountant
1 for the Company Secretary.
Two parcels, one CF, for the stockroom
Some sums of money were also received, as follows:
By first class mail – cheque for £23, cheque for £4.10, cheque for £36.09. Postal orders for £6, £2, 40p. Two pound notes.
By second class mail postal orders for 40p, 67p, 83p, £4.50.
By registered post – £12 notes, 2 £5 notes, 6 £10 notes.
Sort this mail and note how you would deal with it. Complete any registers necessary. Imagine names and addresses, please.

Post Office
Record Card for Locking Franking Machine

User	Die No
Machine Location Address/Postcode	Telephone No
Controlling Post Office	Setting Office
Posting Points (in addition to setting office)	

Model	Machine/Meter No	Setting Unit	Names on Date Stamp
Machine supplied by			Post Office /

	Payment		Descending Register						
Date	Amount £	Unit Equivalent	Before Setting	After Setting	Ascending Register	Total Settings to date	Set by	Chkd by	Remarks
1	2	3	4	5	6	7	8	9	10

P3341 R20416Z7/77 94m Item Code 482495

Figure 37 A franking machine docket

22 Banking and current account procedures

Receptionists are sometimes required to act as cashiers, particularly if they are employed by such firms as television rental companies or hotels. They will therefore need to be fairly knowledgeable about banking procedures and the use of cheques and credit cards.

There are three parties to a cheque:

The payee   the person named on the cheque and who is to be paid
The drawee   the name of the bank from where the money is to be drawn
The drawer   the person who signs the cheque and who is actually paying out the money.

When presented with a cheque the receptionist should check the following points.

1 *The date* – a cheque may be presented at a bank on or after the date shown on it. Generally speaking, however, cheques are valid for six months and after that period of time they are said to be out of date and may be dishonoured.

2 *The amount* – the amount of money should be written twice, once in words and once in figures and the two amounts should agree. If a mistake has been made then the drawer of the cheque should be asked to correct the error(s) and sign the correction.

3 *The payee* – the payee's name should be correctly written. This is especially important if the payee is a limited company as the words 'and Co Ltd' must appear after the name of the company.

4 *The drawer's signature*

If any of the above items are incorrect then the cheque will be dishonoured and returned to the payee with the reason stated on it eg words and figures differ, and possibly it will also be marked Refer to drawer.

A receptionist who habitually accepted cheques without ensuring that they were correctly drawn

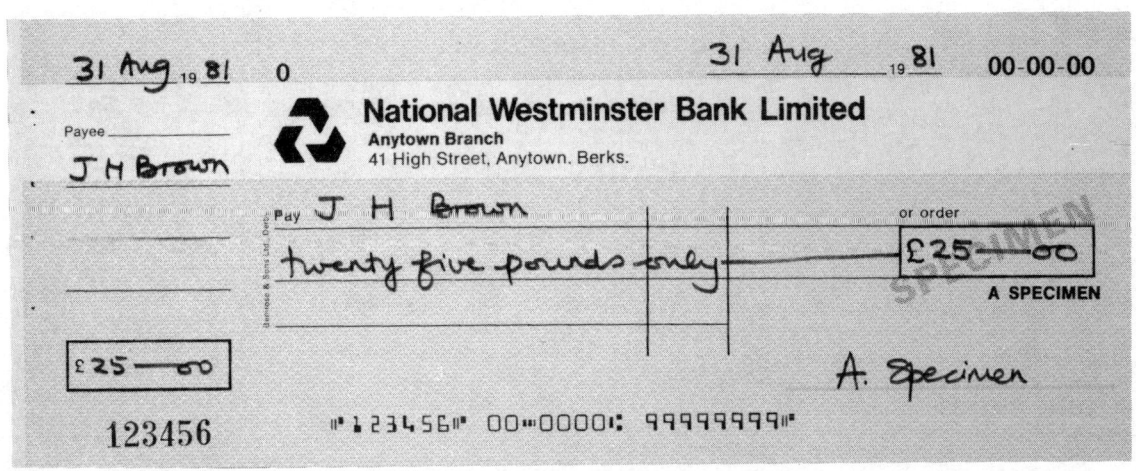

Figure 38   A cheque

would expose her organization to a possible risk of loss.

A receptionist must remember the following points if she has to issue cheques for her firm. On the left-hand side of the cheque is a tear-off portion called a counterfoil which remains in the cheque book. The section remaining is sometimes called the cheque stub and on this should be recorded precise information about the cheque:
a) the date;
b) the amount;
c) the cheque number;
d) the name of the payee.

This information may be employed to trace or stop payment on a cheque. If a cheque is lost or stolen the receptionist may telephone the bank and ask them to 'stop' it, following up this request with written confirmation. She will use the information on the counterfoil so that the bank may identify the cheque in question.

Cheques are usually crossed. This 'crossing' is indicated by two parallel lines either drawn or printed on the cheque. Crossed cheques must be paid into a bank account and, if it is required to be paid into an account in a name other than the payee of the cheque, the cheque should be endorsed on the reverse by the payee. Certain crossings contain certain endorsements and, if in doubt, the receptionist should check the nature and requirements of these with her bank.

The receptionist may need to pay money into her firm's bank account and will use a paying-in book for this purpose. A copy is kept in the book so that a record may be kept of all payments made into the bank. The receptionist should sort the cash into different denominations and the amounts entered into the appropriate column. All cheques and postal orders are listed on the back of the paying-in slip. This aids the bank cashier when checking the money.

Sometimes a receptionist will need to use the night safe. This is a facility offered by the Commercial banks for those depositors who wish to place money in the bank's vaults for safe keeping, after the normal banking hours. The night safe is set in the wall of the bank and the receptionist will be able to unlock it with the use of a key issued by the bank.

At the end of her working day, the receptionist will place all her money, plus a completed paying-in slip in a specially issued wallet or box. The container will be held safely in the bank vaults until the following morning when it is retrieved by members of the bank staff. They will open the wallet and check the cash and cheques against the paying-in slip and the contents will remain under dual control until the check has been completed. The receptionist's organization will have its current account credited with this amount and the receptionist may collect the wallet and counterfoil of the paying-in slip at her leisure.

Frequently cheques are only accepted for small amounts when supported by a cheque card. This card will guarantee a cheque to the value of £50. When the receptionist is presented with a cheque in payment she will ask to see the presenter's

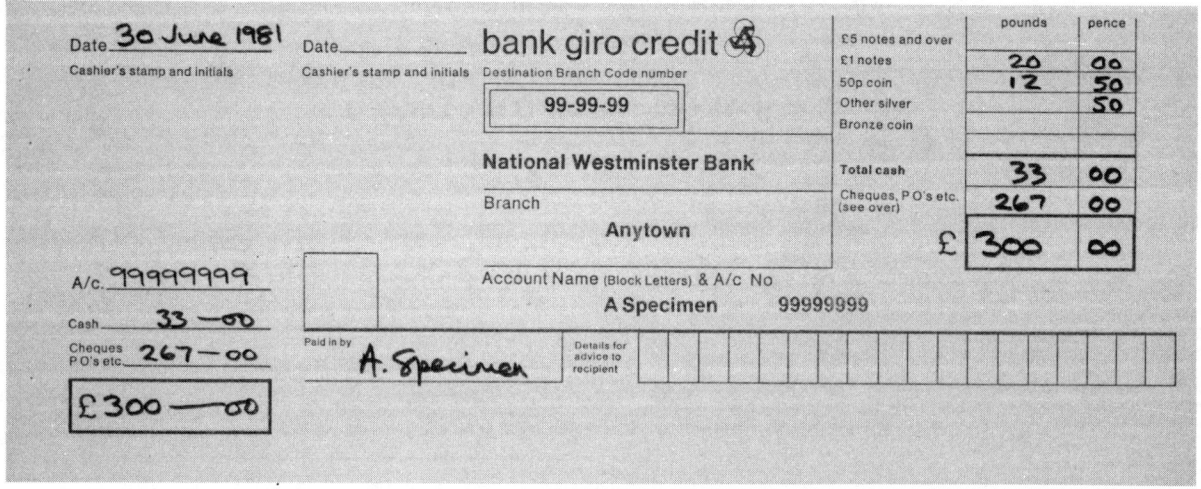

Figure 39 A paying-in slip

cheque card and will fill in the number and any other details which may be required according to the conditions controlling the use of such a card. Credit cards are becoming increasingly popular in paying accounts and in purchasing goods and services. In this case, as it is payment in itself, the receptionist follows whatever instructions given by that particular credit card company in respect of completing the credit transaction ie using the credit card machine with the appropriate stationery and getting the customer to sign the credit card slip. The credit card centre will reimburse the organization for the amount. The credit card holder will receive a statement at the end of the month showing the amount of money owing to the credit card centre. This is an extremely easy and convenient way to pay for goods and services.

At regular intervals the bank will send a bank statement showing the amount of money held in the organization's current account. A bank statement is an account from the bank showing all the transactions that have taken place between a bank and its clients since the last statement was issued. It shows all the money paid out of the current account and all the money that has been paid in. Sometimes a receptionist's cash book may not agree with the bank statement and she must then draw up a reconciliation slip. This will

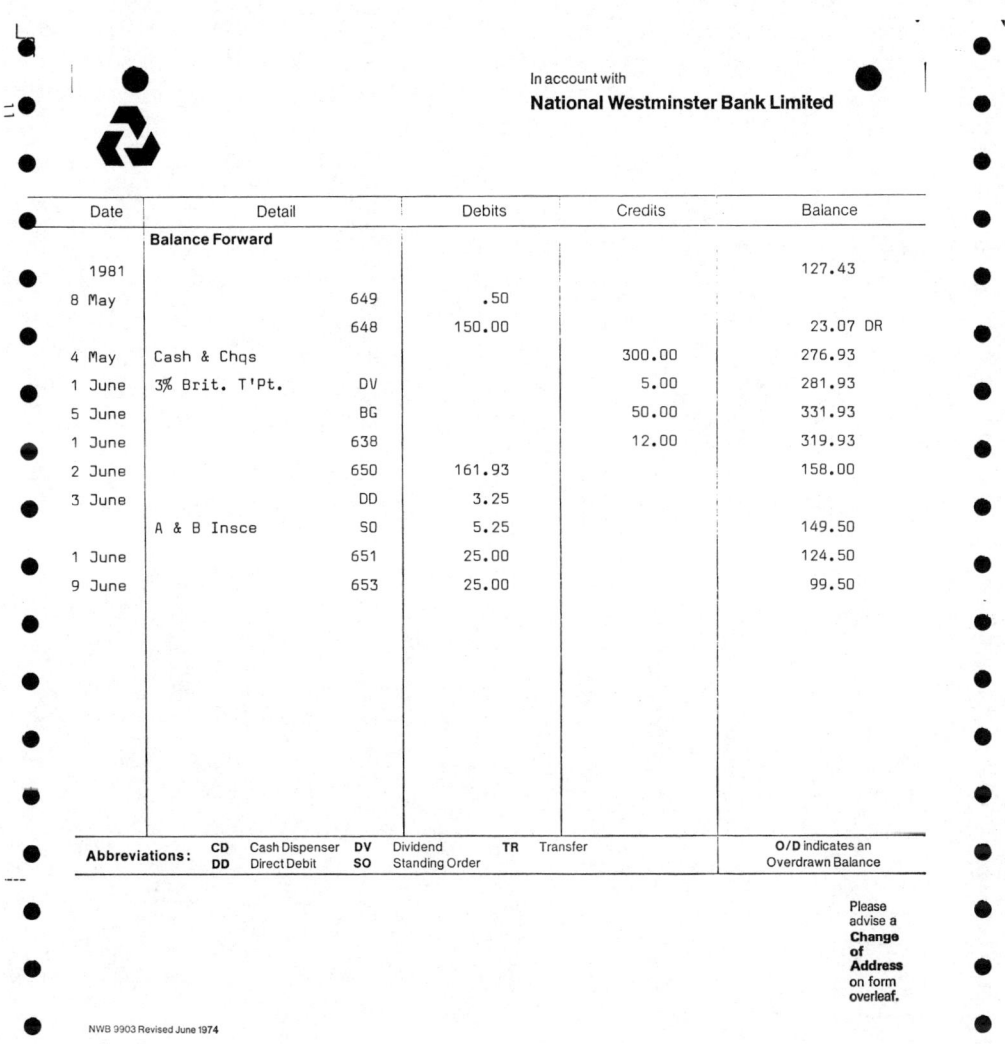

Figure 40   A bank statement

reconcile the bank statement with her own records. The difference is usually due to credits paid in at branches other than where the account is maintained. Cheques may also have been sent to creditors in payment of bills which have not yet been presented and not yet debited to the firm's current account.

Questions

1. Who are the three parties to a cheque?
2. What points should a receptionist watch for when presented with a cheque in payment?
3. What information should be given to the bank when a receptionist wishes to 'stop' a cheque?
4. What is
   a) a general crossing
   b) a special crossing?
5. What is a night safe and why is it so useful to the business person?
6. Why does the receptionist need to sort her cash into different denominations when paying money into the bank?
7. What is the difference between a cheque card and a credit card?
8. What does 'reconciling a bank statement' mean?

Assignment 15

1. Count the envelope of cash given to you (Note – each student is being given a different amount of cash in her/his envelope).
   The following cheque and postal orders were also received as remittances in your firm's morning post:

		£
Bennetts & Co	Cheque	29.80
James Gleddon	Cheque	2.93
J Andrew	Postal Order	.82
A Smithers	Postal Order	1.80

2. By completing the appropriate forms, show how the above monies could be paid in by yourself to the credit of Falmouth Technical College Ltd, Killigrew St Falmouth, dated 26.4.1981,
   a) at their local bank (Midland) A/c No 158340
   b) At their local post office A/c No B2 339 1483.

3. Complete a third form to pay the same money to the credit of the Eastern Branch of your firm (Fal Tech etc) at Reading. The Eastern Branch of the firm have an account at the High Street Branch, Reading A/c No 158392 (dated 26.1.81).

4. The Eastern Branch pay their office staff by credit transfer once a month. Prepare bank giro credits for the following employees:
   Mr J Jones who banks at the same place as his firm (Code No 21-08-49) account number 129843.
   Mrs Spence who has the same bank but the Upton Branch, Reading (Code 29-84-32) (Account No 824379).
   Mrs Dancer and Miss Shoebury who both bank at Lloyds, Church Parade, Reading (Code 21-70-39) Accounts 889432 and 921379 respectively.
   Mr Stonevear and Mr Cosgrove who bank with the Whiteknights branch of National Westminster, Reading (Code 20-84-32) Accounts 721842 and 701020.
   The authorisation is to be signed by yourself as Chief Accountant and dated 26th January 1976.
   The amounts concerned are as follows:

J Jones	£280.93
K Spencer	200.42
V Dancer	182.89
IM Shoebury	143.29
J Stoneyear	275.20
BA Cosgrove	300.19

5. Two other members of staff are paid by cheque, Mr AB Sinclair and Mrs C Benham, £240.83 and £200 respectively. Sign and draw cheques on behalf of the firm as Chief Accountant, dated 26th January 1976. The cheques should be crossed A/c Payee only.

6. Sign and draw a cheque to cover the total amount of the credit transfer schedule, made payable to the bank, and crossed.

23 Petty cash

In some organizations the receptionist is responsible for dealing with the petty cash.

A busy cashier will not want to bother with small items of expenditure such as 35p for sugar and 85p for bus fares. She or he will find it an irritating waste of time and so will allocate a certain sum of money to be used for the petty cash.

The receptionist will handle the petty cash float and hand out cash for small items of expenditure. She will need to be aware of exactly what is spent and must keep careful records. It is very easy to lose small sums of money through loss or pilfering if these records are not precise and accurate.

Each time that an amount of cash is required for a purchase, such as coffee, then a petty cash voucher is completed by the receptionist. Notice that the petty cash voucher is numbered for precise identification. The date, the money spent and the item on which the money has been used is entered onto the petty cash voucher. Each one is signed twice, once by the person spending the cash and again by the receptionist. This means that she checks the expenditure and so avoids fraud, loss and misuse of the petty cash account.

The float must be kept in a special petty cash box which locks. The petty cash box must be placed in the safe at night or, failing the use of a safe, it must be locked away in a cupboard or a drawer. The completed petty cash vouchers should be filed in numerical order, using a ring or lever arch file for storage.

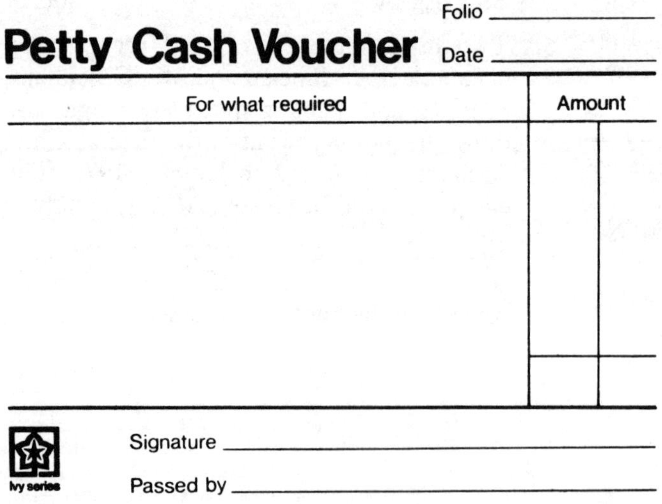

Petty Cash Voucher Folio _____ Date _____

For what required	Amount

Signature _____
Passed by _____

Ivy series

Figure 41   A petty cash voucher

A check of the petty cash may be made at any time by adding the completed vouchers together totalling the cash spent. This must be subtracted from the original amount allocated for the petty cash float. This figure should equal the amount of cash contained in the petty cash box.

At regular intervals the receptionist should enter the petty cash vouchers into the analysis sheet of the petty cash book. There is no set interval for doing this. She may prefer to do it every day or make time once a week for it. It is better that she has a regular routine for this as, if the petty cash has a large call upon the float, she may find it very time consuming, a task that will take hours of her valuable time if the book keeping is left to the end of the month. Apart from the time it will take, it is far more difficult to trace missing vouchers or to balance the account.

An analysis sheet is used to keep a record of all the money spent according to the petty cash vouchers and the balance at the end of the month. The receptionist takes it at precise intervals, say the last Friday of each month, to the cashier for verification. He or she will check that the petty cash account balances and will repay to the receptionist the money that has been spent on the original float. This method of repayment to bring the petty cash float back to the original amount is called the imprest system.

The advantage of using analysis sheets for petty cash is that it can be seen at a glance exactly how much has been spent on, say, post during the accounting period.

The analysis sheets are usually filed in date order in a ring file. When all the petty cash vouchers have been entered on to the analysis sheet and checked then they may be destroyed, unless there is a specific enquiry relating to one of the vouchers. The analysis sheets must be kept until the annual audit in case there are any queries on the final balance sheet for the year.

Example

The float for November was £40.00 and the following amounts were spent on petty cash.

Voucher number	Date	Details	Amount
152	2	Stamps	5.00
123	3	Taxi fares	1.20
154	4	Flowers for recep.	1.85
155	9	Tea	0.70
156	10	Biro refills	0.45
157	12	Envelopes	0.36
158	13	Bus fares	1.16
159	14	Window cleaner	7.20
160	15	Taxi fares	0.45
161	21	Coffee	0.98
162	22	Stamps	5.00
163	24	Typing eraser	0.25
164	27	Postal order	1.20
165	28	Milk bill	3.80
166	30	Bus fares	0.84
167	30	Stamps	5.00
168	30	Sugar	0.35

Questions

1. What is the sum of money given to the petty cashier for small purchases called?
2. Why should a petty cash voucher be completed each time a purchase is made?
3. What information should be entered on the petty cash voucher?
4. Where should the receptionist keep the petty cash money?
5. How can the receptionist make a spot check on the petty cash?
6. What is an analysis sheet?
7. What is the imprest method of dealing with petty cash?
8. How would the receptionist file
   a) petty cash vouchers and
   b) petty cash analysis sheets?

Assignment 16

1. You are in charge of the petty cash for your firm. Below is a list of the items of petty cash expenditure during the month of November. Fill out the petty cash vouchers accordingly, making sure that you number and date them. Make up signatures for the person being issued with the money and countersign them yourself.

November 1st	Postage stamps	£5.00
November 3rd	Bus fares	00.75
November 9th	Stationery	£2.21
November 10th	Flowers for the waiting room	£1.65
November 13th	Bus fares	£1.00
November 15th	Milk bill	£3.88
November 20th	Stationery	£4.22
November 29th	Taxi fare	£2.35

2. Rule up a page of a petty cash book. Decide on the size of the float necessary and then enter all the above vouchers in the book. Balance the book at the end of the month. Answer the following questions:

   a) Why are petty cash vouchers issued?
   b) Why are petty cash vouchers numbered?
   c) How are petty cash vouchers filed?
   d) How should the petty cash money be kept safe?
   e) How can the Accounts Department of your firm ensure that the petty cash is being kept properly?
   f) How much cash should there be in the petty cash box on:
   (i) November 4th and (ii) November 19th?
   g) If, when checking the petty cash at the end of the month, you found that you were £5.00 short, what would you do about it?

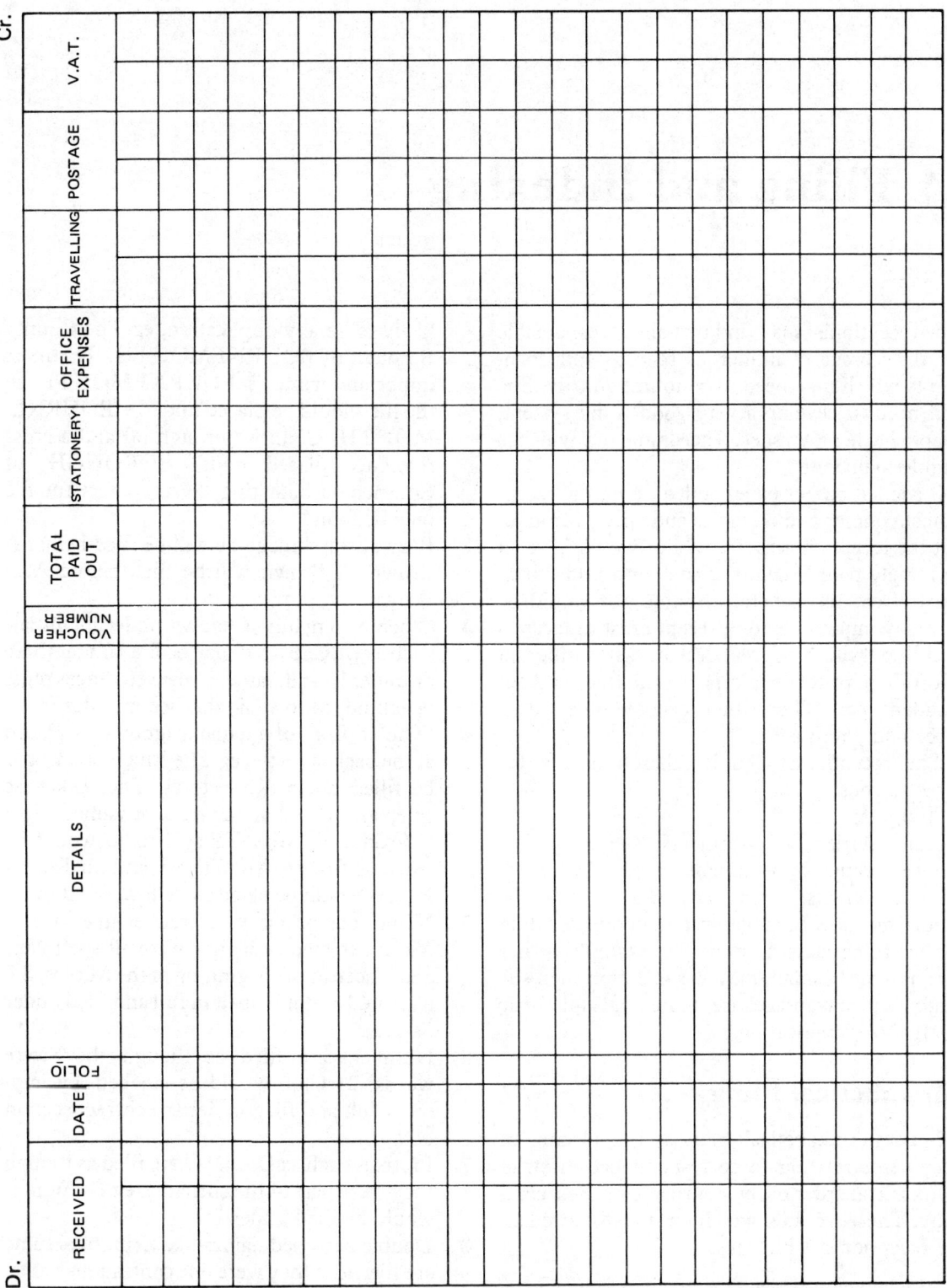

Figure 42 A petty cash analysis sheet

24 Filing and indexing

The receptionist may find that she is responsible for the storage of numerous records and documents which may need to be found quickly. She will need to develop a very good filing system, adapted to her own special needs and one which is simple to operate.

If she left all her papers piled up on the receptionist counter and on tables and chairs throughout the reception area, the visitor would have an extremely poor opinion of such an untidy firm. Apart from the general untidiness it would be virtually impossible for a receptionist to locate a document without a great deal of wasted time and effort. The papers could fall to the floor and get trodden upon. They would become dusty, dog-eared and crumpled.

The receptionist should, therefore, file for three reasons:
1 tidiness;
2 rapid retrieval of documents;
3 preservation of documents.

The receptionist must take into account the requirements of her organization before deciding on her filing classification. For example, if her firm is a fairly small, local organization then she might, with advantage, use the general alphabetic method of classification.

Alphabetical filing

General alphabetical filing is the placing of documents relating to correspondence in strict alphabetical order of their surname or their company. There are rules which must be followed by the receptionist which are:

1 In general it is the best policy to pick out the most important name in a title and file under that. Cross references must be made if there is likely to be any duplication, eg The County Borough of BOURNEMOUTH. The most important name is BOURNEMOUTH so the file should be placed under – BOURNEMOUTH, County Borough of: and a cross reference placed under BOROUGH, of Bournemouth, stating exactly where the file may be found.
2 Brown, standing alone will be filed before A Brown. A Brown will be filed before Alan Brown.
3 When a company is known under its initials such as BBC, BRS it may be filed under these or under its full name. Cross references must be employed to avoid duplicating files.
4 'The' in front of a name is ignored or placed at the back of a title, eg The Ritz Hotel would be filled under Ritz Hotel, The. Likewise titles are placed at the back of names when indexing, eg Miss Tansy Brown would be listed as Brown, Miss Tansy and Sir Robert Pellow would be listed as Pellow, Sir Robert.
5 Names beginning with prefixes like Mac or Mc are treated as if they were all spelt Mac and placed at the beginning of the M files. ST is treated as if it is spelt in full and filed under Saint.
6 Numbers are filed as though they were words. 21 Club would be labelled Twenty-one Club and filed under the correct section of T.
7 Prefixes such as De and O are filed as though they were part of the surname, eg De Winter would be filed under D.
8 Double barrelled names like Crumble-Hume are filed as if they were one continuous name, eg Crumblehume.

Alphabetical filing has the great advantage that it

is a direct classification. The receptionist who wishes to find a document from Mills & Brown can go directly to her filing cabinet and extract the relevant file. She does not have to consult an index to discover what the file is numbered.

Large alphabetical systems tend to become cumbersome because of the large number of files needed for common names. It is also very difficult to locate *one* Mr Brown when there is a file full of Mr Browns.

If the receptionist works for an organization such as an advertising agency or an architect then she might find that filing by subject would be more appropriate. The subjects are filed in strict alphabetical order and might look something like this in an architect's office:

Subject filing

Abingdon school	Exterior
	Interior
	Gymnasium
	Sports hall
	Youth wing
Foxglove hall	Annex
	West wing
Grove hospital	Nurses' quarters
	Operating theatre
	X-ray department

If the receptionist is employed by an organization with branches in other parts of the country then she may decide to keep her files in geographical order so that all the correspondence from one specific branch might be grouped together.

Geographical filing

Berkshire	Ascot	
	Newbury	High Street
		Market Road
	Reading	Oxford Road
		Valley Square
Buckinghamshire	Aylesbury	Rollright Street
	Buckingham	High Street
	High Wycombe	Jewry Street
		Broad Street

As with general alphabetical and subject filing the geographical method is indexed in strict alphabetical order.

Numerical filing

If the receptionist has a fairly large filing system to contend with then the numerical system would be suitable. Files are numbered and placed in strict numerical order. Files classified numerically are extremely easy to expand as new files are just added to the back of the existing ones. The receptionist will also find that it is easier to locate and store any file classified in this manner. There is one disadvantage which is that an index must be employed to find the file numbers of specific correspondents. This may be obviated by quoting the relevant file number as a reference on the top of all correspondence.

The receptionist will need some equipment in which to store her documents. There are three types of filing cabinet:

1 A vertical filing cabinet is fitted with three or four drawers. The documents are filed from front to back hanging suspended from racks within the drawers.

2 Lateral filing is the suspending of files on special rails and filing them from left to right. Lateral filing cabinets are usually cupboards or open shelving and have the advantage over vertical filing cabinets in that they take up a great deal less space.

3 If the receptionist works for a builder or an architect then it might well be that she will have to store large plans or blue prints. In this case she will need a **horizontal filing cabinet** with shallow drawers. The documents are laid flat and filed one on top of the other.

The receptionist may find that some papers such as invoices and petty cash vouchers are easily stored in ring or lever arch files. These may be stored on shelves and provide rapid reference when filed in strict numerical or chronological (date) order.

Indexing

Filing is the storage and retrieval of documents, letters, reports, statistics etc. The receptionist may also need to keep records which is the storing of information on record cards. For instance a receptionist in a television rental showroom would not need to store documents, but she would need to have a record of all her customers, their names, addresses, records of payments, date the rentals are due, reference numbers of the televisions etc. In this case she would make out a record card for each customer and file it so that it was easily accessible.

There are four ways to store record cards:

1 Vertical Card Index
Information is recorded on index cards with the most important information at the top. The index card is stored upright in small drawers as in a vertical filing system.

2 Visible Card Index
Information is recorded on an index card in the usual way but the most important information is written at the *bottom* of the card. This bottom edge is covered with plastic film which ensures that it does not become indecipherable. This bottom edge is known as the visible edge and it has a tremendous advantage over the vertical card index because the most important information may be seen at a glance.

Visible cards may be stored in trays horizontally and also in visible record binders. They may also be stored vertically on swinging panels.

3 Rotary indexes
Here the index cards are placed on wheels which will revolve and enable any card to be rapidly located. Projecting guide cards may divide the index cards into small sections for rapid and easy location.

4 Strip indexing
This looks just like a visible index but does, in fact, consist of only a number of card strips. This is for one-line information only. Very useful for the receptionist for:
   a) telephone numbers/telex numbers;
   b) names and addresses of customers;
   c) sales reference numbers and gradings;
   d) an index for a numerical filing system.

As with visible cards it is easy to locate specific information at a glance, added to which signals may be employed.

Signalling devices are transparent coloured indicators which may be clipped to the visible edge of a visible record card or to the edge of a strip index. Signalling devices draw immediate attention to a specific fact such as a customer placed on the Stop List on a strip index. With visible record cards it is useful to employ signalling devices to show Goods on Order, Goods out of Stock etc.

Another method of keeping records is by employing edge-punched cards. These record cards have the added advantage of rapid analysis of the recorded information. Instead of writing information on a record card the receptionist would use a card with a series of holes punched around the edges. When she wished to indicate a specific item of information she would clip away the relevant hole.

Miscellaneous files

These are kept in the filing system and are used for documents for which there is no specific file. The content of the file should be kept in alphabetical order and a list of the contents should be written on the outside of the file. When six or more related documents are accumulated a special file should be started for them and should be placed in the appropriate place in the filing system.

Cross referencing

A receptionist will sometimes have difficulty in deciding precisely which position one file should take, for example, The National Mutual Co-operative Insurance Society could be filed, logically, under N, M or C. In a case such as this, cross references should be made in *each* of the positions that the file could occupy stating precisely *where* it may be found.

Example – National Mutual Co-operative Insurance, The – SEE Co-operation Insurance, The National Mutual

Absent folders and out cards

It is very annoying indeed when a receptionist needs to spend time searching for a missing file, only to find that it has been removed and not returned to its rightful place.

An absent folder may be used in these cases which gives the name of the file, the date and the signature of the borrower. This will be a check on the precise whereabouts of the file. The absent folder or the out card should be placed in the position usually occupied by the missing file.

Questions

1. Why is it necessary to file?
2. What is
   a) General alphabetical filing
   b) Geographical filing
   c) Subject filing
   d) Numerical filing?
3. How are files stored in the following?
   a) Vertical filing cabinets;
   b) Lateral filing cabinets;
   c) Horizontal filing cabinets.
4. What is indexing?
5. What is a signalling device?
6. What is an edge punched card and why is it so useful to the receptionist?
7. What is a miscellaneous file?
8. Describe the following:
   a) A card index;
   b) A strip index;
   c) A visible card index.

Assignment 17

You are now given customer record slips. The slips are to be used for filing practice, in two different ways.

1 Put slips into strictly alphabetical order of SURNAMES, ignoring counties and towns, for an alphabetical filing system.

Remove the slips which are eighth, sixteenth and twenty-fourth in your pile, but in their places put suitable OUT-CARDS, designed by yourself. Make entries on the out-cards to show that the record slip has today been borrowed by Mr G Edwards of Sales Dept.

Please ask your teacher for a rubber band, and at the end of the exercise use the rubber band to keep your slips together for checking; then put your name on top on a piece of paper held under the band, and hand in.

2 Divide the slips into piles for a geographical filing system in order of the different counties shown on the slips. Then arrange each separate county pile into alphabetical order according to the towns within the counties. Then arrange the customers' names alphabetically within the towns. Then put the set together according to the alphabetical order of counties. Make suitable *guide* slips from the coloured paper or card provided, and put in place.

3 Using the set of follow-up cards which you have already prepared, write up and place into suitable positions the following REMINDERS to be followed-up at appropriate dates, as requested by your boss, Mr A Frampton.

a) 'Make sure that we get Tom Easterbrook's report in plenty of time for the usual Board Meeting scheduled for the 29th of this month' (You like to send out copies of reports in typewritten form with the Agenda fourteen days before the meeting).

b) 'Remind me to book my hotel four weeks in advance for my visit to Manchester on 10th/12th of next month'.

c) 'Don't forget to remind me to get a present and a card for the wife's birthday on the 19th'.

d) 'Do get in touch with Mr Bond's secretary to finalise arrangements for my meeting with him here on the 26th of next month, but better hang on until nearer the date in case the situation changes'.

e) 'Can I rely on you to remind me on Friday afternoon every week to ring and get the weather forecast, then it might give me a better idea of what the weekend weather is going to be like?'

f) 'The sales reps should get their travel expenses claims in by the 3rd of every month – can you do something to remind them?'

25 Calculating machines

The receptionist may have to do calculations during the course of her work. She may have to deal with wages and petty cash which will need to be accurately and rapidly dealt with, as well as other routine numerical work.

Clearly many elementary calculations will be performed mentally or by using a pad of paper and a pen but very often calculators and adding machines are advantageous as they are much quicker and accurate if used correctly. Much of the routine numerical work in reception consists of additions and subtractions and for this type of calculation and add-lister is ideal. These are extremely convenient as the tally-roll, which is attached to the back of the machine, gives a checklist of all the numbers entered into the machine.

Add-listing machines are operated either by hand or electrically. Their biggest disadvantage is their unsuitability for calculations involving multiplication and division. Calculators, on the other hand, not only add and subtract but multiply and divide. A very large range of calculators are marketed but there are three main types:

a) manual calculators;
b) electronic calculators;
c) electronic printing calculators.

The manual calculators are usually quite cheap to buy and are easy to handle. They are worked by rotating a handle clockwise for addition and multiplication and anti-clockwise for subtraction and division. Answers to the calculations may be seen in the calculator's display panels instead of being recorded on the tally-roll as on the add-lister.

The electronic calculator performs its calculations electronically. It has the added advantage of being noiseless and more easily moved from one place to another.

Electronic printing calculators give a print out on a tally roll instead of on display panels. This has the advantage of providing a permanent, checkable record of all calculations performed in the same way as the add-lister. The electronic printer calculator combines the advantages of a permanent record with that of a very rapid calculation.

Questions

1. Why are calculators especially useful to a receptionist?
2. What is the biggest advantage of the add-lister?
3. What are the three main types of calculator?
4. What is the main disadvantage of the first two types of calculator?
5. The electronic printer calculator combines the best points of the add-lister and of the calculator. Explain this statement.

Assignment 18

Use of electronic calculators and adding/listing machines

1. Use the electronic calculators provided to answer the following questions.
2. When you have completed the question sheet, use the adding/listing machines to check your answers. If you find any mistakes, correct them. Keep the tally roll and staple it to your answer sheet.
3. On the back of the answer sheet, explain, briefly the advantages to you of using these machines and say which of the two machines you prefer and why.

a) 4969 + 8056 + 99804 + 63342 =
b) 55668 + 81964 + 988769 + 10240 =
c) 56½ + 98½ + 88½ + 10779½ + 79843½ =
d) 3333 + 88888 + 1099 + 6843 − 5321 =
e) £48.90 + £44.53 + £990.01½ + £9532.11½ =
f) £36.28 + £48.99½ + £568.49½ − £379.65½ =
g) £36.28 × 10 =
h) 9864 × 20 =
i) 368 × 44 =
j) 984 × 352 =

26 Wages and salaries

In a small organization the receptionist may be responsible for paying the wages.

There are many ways of calculating wages.

1 Salaries – where the total yearly income is divided into twelve equal payments which is paid during the last week of the month.

2 Fixed weekly wage – this is paid on a Friday morning and is, usually, the same amount of money each week.

3 Commission – this is a bonus paid to salesmen in addition to their basic weekly wage. This is an incentive which encourages them to make greater efforts to sell their company's products.

There are other ways of calculating wages in the manufacturing trades, but usually these are fairly large organizations and the paying of wages is the province of the wages department.

The total amount that the employee earns before any deductions are made is called gross pay. The receptionist must make two deductions from the gross pay. These are called statutory deductions because they must be made by law. They are

a) Income tax and

b) National Insurance.

Income tax

Income tax is deducted each pay day by the receptionist under a system called 'Pay As You Earn' – PAYE. The money that she deducts from the employees gross salary is sent once a month to the tax collectors at the Inland Revenue Offices.

The receptionist will know precisely how much to deduct from income tax because each employee is given a code number by the Inland Revenue according to his circumstances. A code number regulates the amount of 'free pay' that an individual is allowed to earn before tax. The higher the code number the more free pay is allowed and the less tax is paid. When a receptionist is calculating income tax she does so with the help of tax tables.

Tax table 'A' will tell her the amount that is tax free. She will look up the appropriate week number and the correct code number to find the figure for free pay. The free pay is then subtracted from the gross pay to find out what the *taxable pay* will be. Having ascertained the amount of taxable pay the receptionist will then look up this figure in tax table 'B'.

This figure will give the amount of tax payable on the taxable pay. A record of the income tax will be kept on a tax deduction card.

National Insurance

A certain percentage of an employee's wage must be deducted to pay National Insurance. National Insurance payments go to the Inland Revenue together with tax and are used to pay for the Health Service and the State Pension Scheme. National Insurance tables are available which give the exact amount to be deducted according to the gross wage.

Voluntary deductions

Voluntary deductions may be made by the receptionist at the request of the employee. These are in addition to the statutory deductions and may be stopped or changed on the employees' instructions. Voluntary deductions are:

a) Savings;

b) Christmas Club;
c) Holiday fund;
d) Union subscription;
e) Superannuation;
f) Sports and social club subscriptions.

The receptionist must prepare three documents in addition to the tax deduction cards. These are:

1 The payroll lists all the employees she is paying and gives the following information:
a) Precise identification;
b) Total gross wage;
c) Income tax;
d) National Insurance;
e) Voluntary deductions;
f) Total deductions;
g) Calculation of net pay.

2 The individual pay record is a record for each employee in the organization. This is a record week by week of
a) his/her gross wage,
b) his/her total deductions,
c) his/her net pay.

It is essential that the receptionist keeps this record as there may be queries regarding an employee's past pay and deductions.

3 The pay advice slip has the identical information that is contained on the payroll and individual pay record but is printed on a small strip of paper for inclusion in the pay packet. These are used so that the employee knows precisely how much he has earned and how much tax has been paid etc.

The receptionist must make out a cheque for the total amount of the net wages and take it to the cashier for signature. She must send or take it to the bank together with a cash analysis sheet. This will enable the bank cashier to supply her with money in the correct denominations so that the correct change is available for making up the wage packets. When the receptionist delivers the wages she should obtain a receipt for them to prove that she has, in fact, paid each member of the staff.

NOT-CONTRACTED-OUT STANDARD-RATE CONTRIBUTIONS

WEEKLY TABLE

Before using this table please enter "A" in the space provided on the deductions working sheet (P11 New)/pay record (see Instructions)

For employees who are over age 16 and under pension age (65 men, 60 women).

But *excluding* those married women and widows who are liable to pay contributions at the Reduced Rate – see Table B.

(For employees over pension age or for whom form RD 950 is held use Table C in this volume.)

FOR USE FROM 6 APRIL 1981 TO 5 APRIL 1982

If the exact gross pay figure is not shown in the table, use the next smaller figure shown.

Gross pay	Total of employee's and employer's contributions payable	Employee's contribution payable	Employer's contribution*	Gross pay	Total of employee's and employer's contributions payable	Employee's contribution payable	Employer's contribution*
£	£	£	£	£	£	£	£
27.00	5.79	2.09	3.70	52.00	11.21	4.05	7.16
27.01	5.84	2.11	3.73	52.50	11.32	4.09	7.23
27.50	5.95	2.15	3.80	53.00	11.43	4.13	7.30
28.00	6.06	2.19	3.87	53.50	11.53	4.17	7.36
28.50	6.17	2.23	3.94	54.00	11.63	4.20	7.43
29.00	6.28	2.27	4.01	54.50	11.74	4.24	7.50
29.50	6.39	2.31	4.08	55.00	11.85	4.28	7.57
30.00	6.48	2.34	4.14	55.50	11.96	4.32	7.64
30.50	6.59	2.38	4.21	56.00	12.07	4.36	7.71
31.00	6.70	2.42	4.28	56.50	12.17	4.40	7.77
31.50	6.81	2.46	4.35	57.00	12.28	4.44	7.84
32.00	6.92	2.50	4.42	57.50	12.39	4.48	7.91
32.50	7.03	2.54	4.49	58.00	12.49	4.51	7.98
33.00	7.14	2.58	4.56	58.50	12.60	4.55	8.05
33.50	7.24	2.62	4.62	59.00	12.71	4.59	8.12
34.00	7.34	2.65	4.69	59.50	12.82	4.63	8.19
34.50	7.45	2.69	4.76	60.00	12.92	4.67	8.25
35.00	7.56	2.73	4.83	60.50	13.03	4.71	8.32
35.50	7.67	2.77	4.90	61.00	13.14	4.75	8.39
36.00	7.78	2.81	4.97	61.50	13.25	4.79	8.46
36.50	7.88	2.85	5.03	62.00	13.35	4.82	8.53
37.00	7.99	2.89	5.10	62.50	13.46	4.86	8.60
37.50	8.10	2.93	5.17	63.00	13.57	4.90	8.67
38.00	8.20	2.96	5.24	63.50	13.67	4.94	8.73
38.50	8.31	3.00	5.31	64.00	13.78	4.98	8.80
39.00	8.42	3.04	5.38	64.50	13.89	5.02	8.87
39.50	8.53	3.08	5.45	65.00	14.00	5.06	8.94
40.00	8.63	3.12	5.51	65.50	14.11	5.10	9.01
40.50	8.74	3.16	5.58	66.00	14.21	5.13	9.08
41.00	8.85	3.20	5.65	66.50	14.31	5.17	9.14
41.50	8.96	3.24	5.72	67.00	14.42	5.21	9.21
42.00	9.06	3.27	5.79	67.50	14.53	5.25	9.28
42.50	9.17	3.31	5.86	68.00	14.64	5.29	9.35
43.00	9.28	3.35	5.93	68.50	14.75	5.33	9.42
43.50	9.38	3.39	5.99	69.00	14.86	5.37	9.49
44.00	9.49	3.43	6.06	69.50	14.97	5.41	9.56
44.50	9.60	3.47	6.13	70.00	15.06	5.44	9.62
45.00	9.71	3.51	6.20	70.50	15.17	5.48	9.69
45.50	9.82	3.55	6.27	71.00	15.28	5.52	9.76
46.00	9.92	3.58	6.34	71.50	15.39	5.56	9.83
46.50	10.02	3.62	6.40	72.00	15.50	5.60	9.90
47.00	10.13	3.66	6.47	72.50	15.61	5.64	9.97
47.50	10.24	3.70	6.54	73.00	15.72	5.68	10.04
48.00	10.35	3.74	6.61	73.50	15.82	5.72	10.10
48.50	10.46	3.78	6.68	74.00	15.92	5.75	10.17
49.00	10.57	3.82	6.75	74.50	16.03	5.79	10.24
49.50	10.68	3.86	6.82	75.00	16.14	5.83	10.31
50.00	10.77	3.89	6.88	75.50	16.25	5.87	10.38
50.50	10.88	3.93	6.95	76.00	16.36	5.91	10.45
51.00	10.99	3.97	7.02	76.50	16.46	5.95	10.51
51.50	11.10	4.01	7.09	77.00	16.57	5.99	10.58

*For information only. DO NOT ENTER ON DEDUCTIONS WORKING SHEET (P11 NEW).

Figure 44   P11

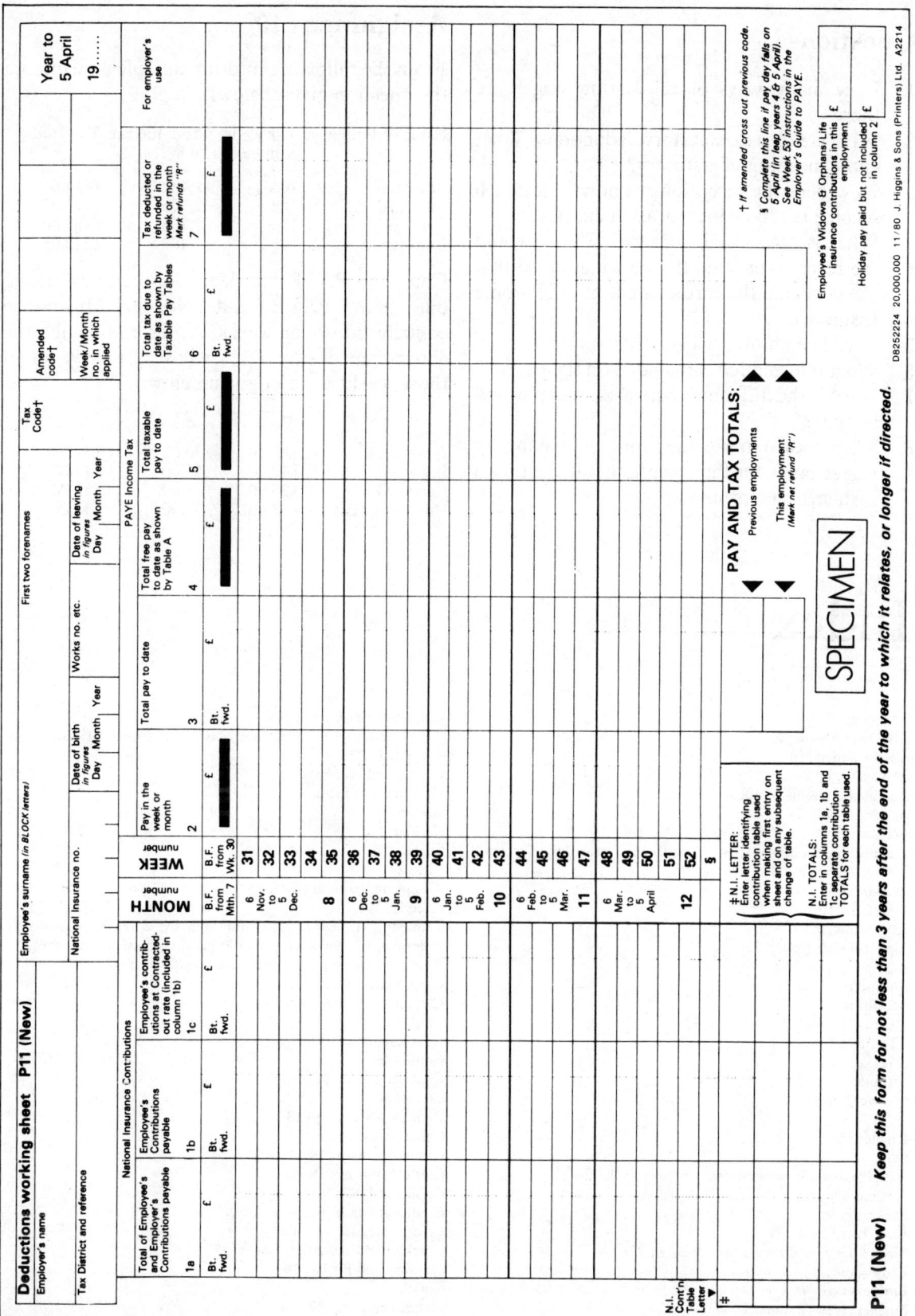

Figure 45 National Insurance table

Questions

1. How many ways of calculating wages are there?
2. What are the two statutory deductions? What is the meaning of statutory?
3. How does the receptionist know how much income tax to deduct for each employee?
4. What is National Insurance? Where would the receptionist find the information so that she deducted the correct amount of National Insurance?
5. Give five voluntary deductions.
6. What information is included on the payroll?
7. What is the difference between gross pay and net pay?
8. Why does it make the work of making-up wages easier for the receptionist if she uses a cash-analysis form?

Assignment 19

From the following information, please work out the question given below:

Name of Employee	Tax Code Number	Gross Income To Week 38	Tax Paid
Adams, C.	106	£1,482	£244.65
Baker, A.	168	£1,506	£126.35
Carter, G.	170	£1,786	£187.40
Donovan, Miss M.	115	£1,482	£222.05

Complete PAYE tax deduction cards (working out both PAYE and National Insurance contributions) for weeks 39, 40 and 41 for the above-named employees whose gross wages in those weeks were as given below:

	Week 39	Week 40	Week 41
Adams, C.	£38.00	£40.00	£34.00
Baker, A.	£42.00	£40.00	£45.00
Carter, G.	£28.00	£48.00	£52.00
Donovan, Miss M.	£38.00	£39.00	£40.00

Index

AA book, 22
ABC travel books, 22
Absent folders, 98
ADC calls, 60
Add-listing machines, 100
Accident book, 53
Accidents
   collisions, 52; danger spots, 52; falls, 52; overloading, 52; report form, 55–6; step ladders, 52
Accountants
   cost, 18; financial, 18
Alarm calls, 61
Alphabet code (telex), 77
Answering sets, 66
Anti-perspirants, 3
Appointments
   cards, 33; diaries, 32; books, 32–3
ATLAS, 67
Atlas, 22
Attitude, 6
Awkward callers, 9, 11

Balance sheet, 18
Bank
   night safe, 88; paying-in slip, 88; reconciliation slip, 89; statement, 89
Bar chart, 36
Black-listed callers, 9
Black's Titles and Forms of address, 9, 22
Body odour, 3
Business card, 7
Business News Summary, 30, 60

Calculating machines, 100
   add-listing, 100; electronic, 100; electronic printing, 100; manual, 100
Card callmaker, 66
Cash analysis form, 93
Cash book, 89
Cashier, 18
Ceefax, 26
Cheese
   blue, 46; hard, 46; soft, 46
Cheques
   amount, 87; card, 88; counterfoil, 87; date, 87; drawee, 87; drawer, 87; endorsements, 88; general crossing, 88; payee, 87; refer to drawer, 88; special crossing, 88; stopped, 88
Chiropodist, 3
Claiming lost property, 14–15
Clothing, 3
Coat stand, 14
Coffee, 46
Collecting mail, 84
Conversation, 6
Company Secretary, 18
Compuphone, 67
Cost accountant, 18
Cost accounting, 18
Credit card, 89
Credit card calls, 61
Credit note, 48
Crockfords' Clerical Dictionary, 23
Customs and Excise, 29
Cuticles, 2
Current account, 87

Daily Telegraph, 29
Dandruff, 2
Date stamp, 82
Decor, 14
Delivery note, 48
Deodorants, 3
Dental register, 23
Departments, 17
　administration, 18; accounts, 18; finance, 18; marketing, 19; personnel, 19; production, 19; purchasing, 20
Dialling codes, 70, 72
Dialling tones, 70–1
Diary, 32
Dictionary, 21
Directors, 17
　board of, 17; executive, 17; part-time, 18
Directory enquiries, 72
Directory of Directors, 22
Directory of Manufacturers, 22
Discretion, 12
Doctors' appointments book, 7
Drawee, 87
Drawer, 87

Electronic calculators, 100
Electronic printing calculators, 100
Embassies, 29
Emergency services, 60
Employees' responsibilities, 53
Employers' responsibilities, 53
Enclosures, 82
Eye make-up, 3
Eyebrows, 3

Feet, care of, 3
Filing
　absent folders, 98; alphabetical, 96; cross referencing, 98; geographical, 97; horizontal, 97; lateral, 97; miscellaneous, 98; numerical, 97; out cards, 98; rules for, 96; subject, 97; vertical, 97
Finance accounting, 18
Financial accountant, 18
Fire
　drill, 52; electrical, 52–3; escapes, 52; precaution, 52; prevention, 52
First aid
　bleeding, 57; burns and scalds, 57; certificates, 57; confidence, 57; fainting, 57; fractures, 57; hospitals, 57; mouth-to-mouth rescusitation, 57; pain, 57; pressure points, 57; shock, 57; wounds, 57
First class mail, 82
First impressions, 1
Fixed time calls, 61
Flower arrangement, 42
Fowler's Modern English Usage, 21
Franking
　dockets, 84–6; machines, 84; regulations, 84
Freefone, 61

Gazetteer, 22
Goods received note, 49
Grooming, 1

Hair, 2
Halitosis, 4
Hands, care of, 2
Hotel register, 8
Hotel registration card, 8
Hygiene, 3

IDD, 60
Income tax
　code number, 102; deduction card, 102; free pay, 102; PAYE, 102; tax tables, 102
Indexing
　edge punched cards, 98; rotary, 98; signalling, 98; strip, 98; vertical card, 98; visible card, 98
International Who's Who, 22
Introduction
　examples, 9; rules, 9

Job centres, 30

Kelly's Directory, 22

Law list, 22
Line graphs, 25
Loudspeaking telephones, 66
Lost property
　book, 15; claims, 14–15; cupboard, 14–15
Loyalty, 12

Magazines, 9
Mail
　collecting, 84; first class, 82, 84; private, 82; recorded, 82; registered, 82; second class, 82; weighing, 84
Make-up, 2
Management, 17
Manual calculators, 100
Medical Directory, 22
Memoranda, 77
Messages, 49
Messengers, 49
Monitoring calls, 71
Motoring information, 60
Municipal Year Book, 23

Name tags; 6
Nails, care of, 2; varnish, 2
Navy, Army and Airforce Lists, 22
National Insurance, 102
　table, 105
Net pay, 102
Night safe, 88

Office Manager, 18
Office organization, 10
Oracle, 26
Organization charts, 17, 18, 19, 76
Out cards, 98

P11, 104
PABX, 65
Paging device, 66
Pay advice, 103
PAYE, 102
Payee, 87
Pay record, 103
Pay roll, 103
Parcels
　checking, 48; receiving, 48
Paying-in slips, 88
PBX, 64
Personal calls, 61
Personnel officer, 19
Petty cash,
　analysis sheet, 93, 95; filing, 93; float, 92; vouchers, 92
Photocopying, 83

Pie charts, 37
Pigeon holes, 83
Planning telephone calls, 71
PMBX, 65
Pocket paging, 66
Post book, 83
Post Office Guide, 21
Posture, 1
Prestel, 26
Problems, 11
Production Manager, 20
Protocol, 11
Public address system, 66
Public relations, 45
Purchasing Manager, 19

RAC handbook, 22, 30
R/D (return to drawer), 88
Reception register, 6–7
Recorded delivery, 82
Reference books, 21, 30
Registered mail, 82
Remittances, 82
Remittances book, 82
Roget's Thesaurus, 21
Routing slip, 83

Safety at Work Act, 52
Salaries, 102
Sales representatives, 10
Second-class mail, 82
Security
    documents, 13; personnel, 13; valuables, 13
Shampoos, 2
Sherry, 45
Shoes, 3
Skin care, 2
Staff responsibility, 52
STD, 60
Stock Exchange Year Book, 22
Strip index, 72, 98

Tact, 10
Tape callmaker, 67
Telegrams
    confidential, 80; costing, 79; forms, 79; greetings, 80; messages, 79; multiple, 80; overnight, 80; overseas, 80; pre-paid, 80; priority, 80; telephoning, 79; telexing, 79

Telephone
    alphabet, 71; call charges, 60, 62, 69; conversations, 74; credit cards, 61; code numbers, 72; correct dialling, 70; cross reference lists, 76; dialling tones, 70; directories, 72; disconnection, 70; equipment: answering set, 66, ATLAS, 67, card callmaker, 66, compuphone, 67, intercommunication, 67, paging device, 66, tape callmaker, 67; manner, 69; messages, 70; monitoring, 71; planning messages, 71; routing calls, 74; services: ADC, 60, alarm call, 61, business news, 60, credit card, 61, emergency, 60, fixed time, 61, Freefone, 61, motoring, 60, personal, 61, the time, 60, transfer charge, 61; techniques, 69; tones, 71; wrong numbers, 70
Teleprinters, 77
Teletext, 26
Telex
    advantages, 78; code, 77, 79; directory, 78; disadvantages, 78; operation, 77–9; punched tape, 77; transmission, 77
Tickler file, 39
Time, 60
Tourist office, 30
Trade delegation, 29
Trade journals, 30
Transfer charge calls, 61
Travel agents, 29

Viewdata, 26
Visitors
    black listed, 9; with appointments, 7, 9; without appointments, 9
Visual aids, 35
Visual control boards, 39
Visual planners, 39
Voluntary deductions, 102

Wages, 102
Wall charts, 35
Welcoming visitors, 1, 6
Weighing mail, 84
Whitaker's Almanack, 22
Who's Who, 22
Who Was Who, 22
Willing's Press Guide, 23
Wines
    fortified, 45; red, 45; rosé, 45; serving, 45; sherry, 45; sparkling, 45; white, 45

Yellow Pages, 21
Youth Employment Centres, 30